The Spiritual Medicine - The Power of Success

Herman Wong

PublishAmerica
Baltimore

First printing   !

PublishAmerica has allowed this work to remain exactly as the author intended, verbatim, without editorial input.

ISBN: 1-60813-186-6
PUBLISHED BY PUBLISHAMERICA, LLLP
www.publishamerica.com
Baltimore

Printed in the United States of America

The Spiritual Medicine

The Power of Success

• *The Universal Law of Success and the Law of Magnetic Energy combines to give us all the power that we need to accomplish many amazing things. If we determine to do small jobs, we may only achieve small results, but if we have a strong desire to do greater work in an enormous way, then our actions determine our results. Nonetheless, both of these actions are driven by our Inner Source and are applicable and directed by you.*

• *All things have the potential to achieve results, only if you believe it is real and have absolute faith in yourself. Actually, it is the power triggered in your subconscious mind empowering a particular thought energy, that guides you to take the initiative and the action required, and is subsequently activated by the Universal flow of life, therefore everything is capable of transmuting from formless into form to obtain a desirable result.*

• *The more positive your thought is it is easier to make a conscious connection to the magnetic energy forces around you.*

The Spiritual Medicine -
The Power of Success

The positive inner-dialogue that we have with ourselves is very powerful and influential, because it uses the subliminal power of the subconscious mind to facilitate the transformation, navigate and generate support, and lead us to succeed and live a peaceful and joyful life. We believe that we shall become...

"I say yes to success!"

Table of contents

Blessings,
Herman Wong

Interview

As you tap into the sacred place of the Unknown and know the unlimited power of your Source. It banishes self-doubt and being still can take you to that awareness.

Opening: This interview was conducted in the summer of July 2005. The conversation was communicated by sensing the subtle energy. However, I felt a two way communication between the spirit and me. Here is the full transcript of my connection with the direct voice of the spirit. At that time, I spoke in silence and I then received an answer from the spirit. I conveyed my current situation, and concern and sensed the answer from the spirit.

Me: When I create an image into an invisible field, I am aware of what it is I desire to manifest inside me and achieve results, and for the good of all. Based on this concept I wrote this book with sincerity. I wish everyone will benefit and experience the knowledge of this book in their lives. I am convinced in my mind that the text (knowledge) contained in this book will bring spiritual awakening to many consciousness souls.

Spirit: Your book has offered a window of opportunity to people to rewrite their own reality and turn turmoil into blessings and success in life.

Me: I hope everyone can shift their present consciousness, and focus on the direction of their passion and true value in reaching feelings of confidence and trust in self and take control of their own dream. I sincerely hope that people will learn and apply the positive thoughts, created by their own spiritual experience by changing their minds and transforming the negative to positive impulses, and turn any shortcomings into everlasting success and works persistently to build peace and prosperous life.

Spirit: For them to recognize and achieve their spiritual power of success it takes patience and trust because success and change cannot happen overnight. However, your book definitely will help them to unlock their unlimited abilities to think better and create their own concept of success.

When you utilize the mind to focus on one point it is much better than scattering your thought on many things at the same time. Mind realization helps you to acquire the desire in life effectively and easily. A conscious mind helps you to understand the cause of ups and downs in life's experience. You recognize and comprehend the root of the problems, you can put all the puzzles and pieces together, and refocusing on the decision to improve your solution and outcome in everyday life.

Spirit: This is especially true, when you recognize the truth in the Universal Laws of Harmony, which create the magnetic force of attracting more of good fortune with a grateful mind. Gratitude allows the acceptance of things just the way they are and let go of control, which in turn vibrates, and projects a greater energy to create a magnetic force resulting in a positive outcome.

Me: I have faith in myself; I dedicate this entire book to the *Divine* and follow my heart's desire, and let *it* lead me to the better part of my journey and make all the right decisions. I trust the Inner Knowing for the best path for me, and I have trust and faith that this will happen and is for the greatest good. I choose to live freely and learn to change the way I experience problems, and respond to life in a loving and peaceful manner. I create and transcend my dreams and desires into the Universe that are uniquely created by me and my thoughts.

Spirit: Life is full of challenges and to explore life you must allow your soul to experience it and continue until your life has been fulfilled. Everything is possible within the silent black hallow place. It is within this secret place you shed all your dreams to light. It is the subliminal mind beliefs that determine and help you to achieve success. Finally, when it comes down to succeeding, the important thing is to eliminate any negative thoughts and continue to hold onto inspired and positive impulses, and this will extinguish the negative energy in the mind and physical body. Continuous focus on eliminating negative attitudes will bring more pleasant moments in your activities and transform your life. Remember your predominant thoughts have all the power to manifest and transmute every dream into actual reality. Take action on what you dream about, and you may suddenly notice there are resources around that you could use and meeting people who could help you, but you did not realize this before. This is your life you know in your heart and soul what's best for you and have done right things.

Spirit: I heard you say, "I want to manifest my book, entitled "THE SPIRITUAL MEDICINE—THE POWER OF SUCCESS" to the Universe."

Spirit: You must be aware when you envision a mental picture into an invisible field, you know what you want to manifest.

Me: It is in my heart's desire that I would like to see my book being published, and transform it into a physical reality.

Spirit: I understand that you desire to publish your book, entitled ***"THE SPIRITUAL MEDICINE—THE POWER OF SUCCESS***" manifest to the physical world from the invisible Universe. You have conveyed and hoped that your book will connect to resonance souls of many people. It is your desire they will benefit and experience the joy of reading and learning from this book. They become fully conscious of their thoughts, which connect to the vibrational harmony of the Universal flow and receive the benefits from their own attractions to the power of success.

Spirit: "Is it correct?"

ME: "Yes, it is right."

Spirit: Ok, then tell me in your experience, and imagine how you want your book to manifest?

Me: Well, I desire it to be published by a publisher and the book will distributed to bookstore's Worldwide.

Spirit: Ok, say if I can give you that, explain to me now, what is in your experience that you feel helps promote your book and its positive effect on others.

Me: I feel so profound and connected to the idea of this book that I have written and described in detail the many ways, which show my life has improved and transformed. I have transformed my life into greater harmony with spiritual and Universal principals. I felt very strongly that my life has been guided through this spiritual process. I have perceived life differently through various perspectives to find and to recognize God. I realize that God is indeed omnipresence and resides in my heart. I am aware that everything I have came from the Universal Source of the Mind of God. It is in me to call on "Him" for assistant. The Source will never interrupt anything without my invitation. I understand that it is a gift nobody can take away from me. The Source joins with me, I know, even before I was born into this planet Earth. It is a gift in the heart. The only condition is I must acknowledge and accept "Him." God is amazing!

Spirit: Tell me, how do you recognize God and His influence on you now? I am sure it can't happen overnight.

Me: It has indeed just happened like that. It really just happens...like a snap of a finger. I would say it has happened without a forewarning or any sign at all. Like an express train approaching you without warning.

Me: It was right after my face surgery to remove the lesions from my face. Immediately after the surgery, I knew that God dwells in me. Joy and bliss started emanating from within. From then on, I believed and accepted His Divine love. I understood the wisdom of the Mighty unknown. His loves is ever lasting and unconditional. Without the surgery, I would have not believed in God.

Spirit: So how do you feel about it now, and have you doubted about what you have found in your journey to find God?

Me: No, I do not have a moment of doubt about it. Period! I accepted it unconditionally. I feel His presence and power in me. I mean, why should I doubt it? It will only help and benefit my life and indeed, it transforms my life to a completely new level. It is what I have been yearning for. All I have done is dedicated my time to God daily. I meditate on God and listen to God speak to me. I am grateful to the Divine Light for everything that I have and thank *Him* for *"His"* assistants and meeting my other needs and desire. (**I thank you the spirit to speak with me and the conversation was end here.**) I believe life is a challenge. I had gone through many difficulties and perplexities before I could see triumph. I have faith in God. I believe everything happens for a reason, and everything happens for the best, there is no reason to feel bad about what has happened. I will not allow fear to overpower me.

You recognize God's presence is full of bliss and happiness. It transforms your life into an insightful feeling and an expression of joy. However, you must be aware of how you feel inside and is different from what you experience externally. We must recognize that what we projected from inside and is how we perceive the world outside. Quite often, we have projected the external world as being brutal, hatred and full of envy and people deceiving each other. Unfortunately, this is how we perceive the external world. However, it does not need to happen this way. That is a general perception of how we perceive this unreal world.

In a real world, in other words, in God's world it is very different from what we could imagine and it is beyond our senses and comprehension. In God's world, we feel tranquil and peaceful. There is no war between each nation, no hatred, and jealousy of each other.

Again, what do we have when we are in God's world—we have peace, joy, and goodness. When you are in Heaven, everything is suddenly all cozy and comfortable, and you are as you were young again—you can breathe better and all your aches and pains just vanish. You can go anywhere you want and everything seems more pleasant.

We shouldn't think of lack and everything is sufficient to meet our needs. Since there are no lacks, therefore it will be no struggle that affects our emotions, feelings, and thoughts. Because of negative feelings and emotions, ideas and desires are not able to enter you. You must generate all positive thoughts that have a higher influence and are close to you to use for your benefit. All these negative thoughts will eventually fade away.

Ok, you ask how this is done. You may argue that we have 60,000 thoughts each day and how are we going to eliminate all negative thoughts that emerge to us without warning. That is not difficult at all. At the beginning, you may notice that it is hard to control your thoughts. I understand our thoughts come naturally without any attention. I agreed with you. However, if you want to control your thoughts you can. Nothing is impossible. Like, if you think of a flower, a red rose that you love, but nothing else. You closed all your thoughts that are not related to red rose. You have one-point of thought—red rose. Imagine what the red rose brings to you. Why do you like a red rose? You like the color red—it is beautiful, the color is distinguishable from other flowers. It is your primary choice for romance. It represents love, joy, and wealth. I know all women love red roses. Lol

Now lets us return to the question how to eliminate or shut down unwanted thoughts that influence your lives. When you are able to close all other thoughts and focus on only one positive thought, you eventually will terminate any negative thoughts that emerge to you. Even, if it appears sometimes, but it will fade out. Most importantly, you have paid no attention to it. When you give no attention it will fade out, because you give it no power. You have made a vow to yourself, "*I closed all negative influences that emerge to me, and I invited the power of God's light to come to me.*" If you do this, all the VISIBLE and INVISIBLE negative influences will be closed off, while all positive higher energies will be attracted and in a sense you have invited this in and they will enter.

In the mind, there is doubt; there is reality.

Negative thoughts can help us to decide otherwise.

Are you in good hands?

I am.

God is real and I can recognize this! The same will apply to your negative attitude. Satan is real and you can eliminate it by shutting the door behind him.

When you take control of your thoughts, you have command of the mind and this will eliminate doubt to bring wonderful things to you, because you have separated the idea of attraction from repulsion. If you let your mind think freely without discipline, then you still experience the full effect of negative ideas. However, if you train your mind to think positive and shut out all negative emotions as soon as they emerge, eventually the mind will only be aware of the positive attraction and maintains the peaceful ally. Therefore, the right mind obeys your will.

When negative thoughts occur they will stay for twelve hours and then they will recur every third day. If you can control your negative thoughts, and shorten them to ten hours or shorter, they begin to recur to you only once a week and by practicing daily prayer, and meditation to help you focus on your thoughts and this will be a great improvement. If you continue with prayer, and meditation you will see great improvement in the flow of your thoughts and eventually all these unnecessary feelings will disappear completely. I am now empty of excessive wandering thoughts and recursive thinking. I am the man and it is my call.

Change your thought; it will change your fate and destiny.

Foreword

In the beginning of the millennium, many people have found spiritual comfort and transformation in their lives. Perhaps they have been looking for these changes for some time, but just don't know where to seek for an answer. We are aware of a supreme power above us and know that we have a soul dwelling in us.

There are so many events happening around the globe, which is a mystery and is unknown. For years we have seen nature change and continue to affect our lives such as global warming, climate changes, earth quake, storms and hurricanes and also many have seen miracles happen in their lives after certain events occurred. These people started looking for new knowledge or improvement to fill in that emptiness in their hearts. They are determined to understand what life is about. They are searching for an answer about who are we and why are we here.

If the year 2005 was the beginning of an era into spirituality, then we saw many changes already taking place in the year 2008. We will continue to seek transmutations in order to improve our lives on Earth. We change when we see something we don't like. We change our thoughts to change our reality. We change to love each other, because God is love. We continue to ask the invisible power of the Universe to watch us and open our hearts to each other. We call on the invisible Mind of God to strengthen our spirits and give us the knowledge and wisdom to face difficulties and confusions in time of crisis. We ask the Mind of God to help us to resolve our problems that we face daily. We seek to understand *Him* so that we can consciously connect with *Him* and feel the silence from within. We seek for *His* love and peace. This is because *He* is love and only moving towards *Him*, that we can live our lives truly.

In this malleable world, we seem powerless when events just happen with no known reason. But, the good news is our experiences can bestow blessings upon us from heaven, that there is *"Inner Wisdom"* that dwells in everyone's hearts, a supreme power that no external force in the physical world can hurt or impale us. It is the *"Inner Wisdom"* that creates every possibility that is manifested from the inner state of mind to the material world. As we consciously become aware of this *"Inner Wisdom"* gradually we take possession of this power and aptitude to bring into manifestation the essentials of our complete peace and growth.

Because, this powerful *"Internal Source"* is an integral part of overcoming any despair and turmoil and guarantees that our difficult times are only part of our journey that will lead to a peaceful place where harmony occurs.

The great success of transformation in life is within you. Nobody can give you that intuitive power of success to achieve and accomplish anything you desire, but come from the *Inner Source* dwelling within you. Indeed, you have already adopted the inborn power prior to you coming to this planet Earth. You simply have to recognize and accept it as part of your infinite being and the laws that govern the *Law of Nature*.

Why do some men automatically realize their successes, ambitions, talents than others? They have no problem of gaining success in their ideas and desires, and can easily transform them into actual reality with or without effort. The secret is in the power of our minds. They know how to use their mind powers to create abundance and attract this to them and overcome obstacles, and transform difficulties into thoughtful triumph. Ultimately, they get what they desire and live an abundant life.

Now we understand the power behind the great successes of these people is the mind's creative power, and actually your power of thoughts. So where does this thought power come from? First, our thoughts and ideas come from the spirit into the subconscious mind then shift this to the conscious mind. The conscious mind directs thoughts into action and the subconscious mind simply produces the results for you. The subconscious mind will not change anything, but simply follows your order and then is sent from the conscious mind. The consciousness always has the power to overrule the final outcome.

Mind power is thought energy. When your creative thought power is fully recognized its effect will be seen as achievable and brilliant. But, to achieve abundant results, everything must be applied orderly and comply with the law that governs the *Law of Magnetic Energy* and the *Law of Nature*. You need to concentrate on one point of thought so that the spirit can help you to succeed. A proper compliance is needed to achieve a result and sought within you, but do not depend on help from outside and when you unhesitatingly meditate your thought within, instantly you feel great and miraculously creative miracles occur.

It is evident; therefore one who succeeded in his own investigation is seeking help from within, but not the external world. One who thrives is seeking knowledge and benefit from the *Inner Source* and refuses to recognize and acknowledge the abundance and benefit, accumulated to them in the material world, but through an understanding of the *Law of Magnetic Energy*—like attracted like.

However, it is true that the mind creates opposite thoughts as well as favorable conditions, when we knowingly or unknowingly visualize scarcity, or any kind of unfavorable limited conditions. We created these limitations; many of us are doing this unconsciously all the time.

The Universe cannot distinguish the difference between positive and negative, but only attracts what you intend on creating. The *Law of Magnetic Energy* will bring the means to you after you submitted your desire to the Universe and completed your order. In other words, *"whatever a man sowed is what he shall reap."*

Success also depends upon recognition of the Laws of Success, and the truth that the mind is the creator of all creations and all your desires in the physical material world. Undoubtedly, nothing can be created prior to us recognizing the power of our mind and then transmuted to the desired effect. When we understand the *Law of Success* and place ourselves in harmony and peace with it, and share its benefits. The *Law of Success* is also in connection with the cause and effect and cannot be ignored this is the meaning of the *Law of Karma*.

We now understand every action there is a definite cause, so that when a given result is desired, it meets with all the conditions and returns the effect to you. It is by comparison that these basic instances with one another are unified until all common factors are seen to be equal.

It is therefore the correct use of thought power that has a great impact in your life. It is important for you to understand that in order to acquire what you desire in life you must be in complete harmony with **The Source**. When you are in alignment with **The Source** your thoughts are more lucid and can tranquil your mind to clearly see the clarity of your thoughts and have the abundance emerge in your life at your command.

Success is not merely happening to a select group of privilege mogul people, but can happen to anyone like you and me. However, you must recognize the resource within the self. When you recognize and acknowledge the innate power then you know that your success is within easy reach. Eventually, you can use and apply the innate power to help yourself and others. You know it is a great mental development for your body, mind, and spirit.

The most powerful force in the Universe is the power of nature. It is the most powerful invisible force in the Universe, and the most powerful force of human beings is this infinite power and the only way the invisible power can be manifested is through the power of thought. Through the power of thought we are connected to **The Source**. Through the power of thought, we exercise our muscles, tissues, nerves brain waves, and the whole physical body is connected and affected. It brings about completed physical change and union of a man.

This is the process by which failures is changed to success, because it is subject to one thought and focus on **The Source** to bring the intended manifestation into alignment. Thoughts of inspiration, harmony, peace, love, courage, are substituted for failure, despair, and disharmony, scarcity, and discord. Thoughts of positive vibration take physical exchange and eliminate the negative energy with the light of **The Source**; all things come to you naturally, automatically and effortlessly. You're no longer swimming upstream, but swim with the flow and see the bright light radiate around you. You have attracted more joyful events, people are willing to offer help to you and you simply exercise the power of your thoughts to make a new change in your environment, circumstances and conditions.

At the end of the day in your heart, in your mind you knew that your day was marvelous, because you have succeeded in manifesting the life you want to live abundantly.

Using your creative power even in the middle of the mist will focus your thoughts to eliminate confusion and negative thoughts to gain entry into your mind. You will see the power of lucid thinking will help you to pass this turmoil and transfer it into the ultimate success and profound triumph. The possibilities are so wonderful, beautiful and so facilitating, the limitless feelings are almost unbelievable. However, when we experience the power within and convey it to the external world, then we begin to defy our previous disbelief and begin to look at things differently and then the things we look at have transformed. As we begin to become aware of these inner powers, we shall surrender to the many possibilities of manifesting what we see in our mind and transfer this to the external world. Many powerful inventions occur, because of the awareness of *Inner Wisdom* and transform into the power of thought and the power of trust and faith transmutes our vision into successful reality.

Now remember every major achievement, accomplishment, invention, wealth begin with an *idea!* So, do not be afraid to accept an idea when it comes to you. You should acknowledge and utilize it to your benefit. No one can guarantee a success unless you take a chance and take some action otherwise you won't get anywhere. If you don't accept your ideas and have complete trust and faith in them, you will not move forward in your success. Therefore, if you believe in your idea it can bring profound fortune to you and do not hesitate and have faith and trust to create it out of understanding that it is for the highest good and for all concerned. Your desire, your intention, your faith, your action, and your reality are the real ingredients that went into the power of your success and nobody can deny it. Success begins with the form of an idea and thought! There are no limits when your thought is put into motion with your mind. Your faith will help to remove limitation. Success is within reach.

When you go to bed, each night and each morning when you get up I want to hear you say, "Everything is going to be truly positive. I am going to have a most marvelous time today!
~The Queen of Hearts~

Introduction

Power is energy, energy is power. The power you can receive and convert into many wonderful experiences and blessed with great material wealth, and spiritual and physical prosperity and ultimately, brings you all the success you deserve. Success is the evolution of power or vibration of thought and brings about the vibrational alignment with **The Source** *in the present to gain one's desires in life. Since your thoughts are vibrations and the Law of Magnetic Energy does attract these influences and gives you the power to respond to these energies, you actually activate them and you can draw anything you desire into your life, love, health, wealth and success. In addition, The Power of Success and the Law of Magnetic Energy will endorse each other, which will bring you more of your creative experience to light. Consequently, you become more successful and start to draw attention, gain respect in your profession and many new channels opens in your horizon, and because of your uniqueness; you have summoned your own truth and reality.*

Before we can reach to the Land of Success from the Land of imagination, first we must create and visualize a mental image in the mind's eye and perceive the conditions and activity necessary for its coming and the success is emerging, because of the power of your intention. When the Wright's brothers in 1903 thought of flying into the sky they had this idea in their minds and tried many attempts and experiments before they had finally successfully flew an airplane into the sky. The first airplane was invented then and to this date, we have gained many experiences in the area of flying and for thirty years **NASSA** has successfully sent each spacecraft from Mercury through to Apollo and afterward there were many space shuttles lifting off into the new ocean of space, which led to the idea of passenger voyages into the outer spaces black Universe. It all happens first, because of an idea and then

27

was conceived in the scientist's own "*IMAGINATION*" by using and developing their own power of creativity, before it becomes a reality. Success does not come easy. Many of our accomplishments have to go through failures prior to reaching a final destination. In order to succeed, we must admit failure, and then we learn to experience bliss and happiness of successes. In fact, failure does not exist, but only success because if we do not give up, there never will be any failure. On the contrary, if we have given up after many attempts of testing our invention we will not only experience disappointment, but also we may not see the glory of being successful in our lives.

Many of our greatest successes and inventions are coming from one big idea through the power of thought and imagination. We create the visualize thoughts in our minds, subsequently extending and broadened that idea and to perceive it very clearly step by step and structure by structure of how each frame work is being implementing to become one's own reality. Without imagination, many of our great works and inventions could not have been created.

You can dream, you can have. It does not matter who you are, where your geographical location is and regardless of your education, race, and cultural background, you can always apply the power of imagination to create anything in your mind and later transform it into physical reality. It marks the beginning of success and many blessings from **The Source** and your power of imagination, which is constantly connected with the power to succeed, is within our reaches.

When you focus on love, health, wealth, and success and imagine all of these flowing toward you. Money is one of the main categories that can bring you where you want to be, the more money that attract, the better the vibrational energy around you, success and abundance will put you into the position of a higher spirit and activate a mode of cooperation leading your intentions to thrive.

If you follow this declaration, you can say it aloud or in silence at any time, "*I intend to feel successful and attract prosperity into my life*" immediately your energy will shift to a higher level, as if what your desire has already

28

manifested and fulfilled. You will continue to experience your vibrational harmony and moving towards many faces of success, and you will state what you are, rather than what is missing.

A person can be very successful, but he cannot take all the credit, but if he thinks he can win it all is one huge mistake. It is because at the end nobody knows and wins it all.

Success in creating something in a group effort because, when you create a visualized picture in your mind's eye flowing through you and transcend it into the invisible Universe. After suspending for some time and later meet with the other, which has the same idea and intent and your willingness to join becomes one powerful force and subsequently the formless form becomes mature, and must return to the physical world and befalls your impulse and successful result. You can imagine that without this one powerful force to help you with this joint venture together with your intention in mind and eventually you will arrive with a well developed plan to reach the result, but it will take a little longer time.

Finally, when you apply the power of success to receive your desire and prosperity, do not forget to keep an open mind and to share your richness you received, so that many will also benefit from your success and abundance. If you can do that, you can ask for greater success to come to you and your rewards will reap benefits and wholeness that completes and fulfills every need.

Chapter One
~The Power to Accept as True—You Can Dream It and You Can Have It! ~

Who does not want to live a successful life? Before you can begin to succeed one need to adjust their thinking patterns with the surrounding environment and dwell with harmony. When you have vibrational harmony in your mind, you can almost be certain that you can achieve anything you can imagine, love, health, wealth and success. You can request for more and dream big about success and abundance—it's there for you and the *Universe* has an unlimited supply for everyone.

In actual reality, what we perceive inside can be projected to the external world. In other words, we simply act on what we have contemplated in our mind without any consideration; we lose sight of our goals. Therefore, you must eliminate and cancel any thought that stands in your way of success because of greed, jealousy, intolerance, revenge and many other negative thoughts, which disrupt your ability for success.

Change your personality and it will enhance your success in many ways. Do you know that some sales representatives are more successful than others and the reason for this is they have a more pleasing and candid personalities and that allows other to see them in their true light? For instance, ten cashiers in the Superstore were opened, but one in particular person that I observed was a very pleasant and had a candid personality.

He is very alert to the needs of each of his customers and extends a warm and welcome approach to everyone that is in contact with him. His personality has enabled him to continue a successful working relationship in his work, which adds success and organization in all his accomplishments and he would be an asset to any company. People buy more merchandize, when they are met in a loving and engaging manner and allows for success for both parties concern. This is because the majority of people do take care to make them feel harmonious inside while doing their shopping there.

In a business world, you are in and you are in to win. Your ability to win business contracts is depended on your power to negotiate and influence others in co-operation with you in the spirit of harmony. You need to develop that pleasing leadership personality, confident and self-control, so that you achieve the best meeting for both concerned and this lead to a better relationship with all contacts during the negotiation period. This will elevate you and others to a position of consensus and success in reaching your objectives.

This is a model of protocol, which you can use to advance and enhance your knowledge in succeeding in business ventures and gain what you desire to see, hear, and receive, and most importantly, people that you negotiate with will agree with you, because they are on the same path with you.

Here are the steps you should pay attention to, if you desire to gain success in your life.

- Your life purpose—what are your aims in claiming your success and how do you plan on using all factors that came together to get you from point A to point B. Your purpose is to aim high and always know what you desire, whether you are in school, in your marriage, or on a campaign trail to run for a higher position in the land. You must use your intelligence, self-images, and the power you already have to influence others. You have a warm character, tolerance, patience, and innate power to achieve and win that position. Remember you are always in to win and see success and abundance, and refuse to allow doubt to enter and never look back. You believe success is your objective and your intention. The purpose of manifestation is to produce the successful results. It is the power of your thoughts, desires, and merges with faith and the innate power that transforms your wildest dreams into reality. Plus you can spot an opportunity; on the contrary you can't lose, but you could win huge.

• Your confidences—You must always trust, believe and have confidence in yourself. Because, when you have confidence in your ability, people will have faith, respect, and honor you and this will eliminate fear and worry of not receiving your recognition. You must eliminate the sum of all fears and believe fear is only an illusion and untrue. You must use your ability to distinguish the difference between egoisms and genuine self-confidence, which is based on Divine knowledge.

When you can generate the appropriate knowledge then you can experiment whether your theory will work, or to observe those whose experiment have produced the desired results and utilize the same technique and applied it. When you speak everyone listens to what you say and that is the power of self-confidence that you summon and access.

• Put into practice saving your money—You must save at least 10% of any earnings for the rainy day. No one can be completely successful without saving money for a difficult time. It is a good habit to always save money for emergency purposes.

• Activate your leadership abilities, showing you are not a follower—you must always initiate your leadership skills to lead others.

• Activate the power of your thoughts—You use your innate power to visualize a picture in your mind's eye and later transcend it into the *Universe* and perceiving a formless substance transforming into form and returning to the physical world becoming your own reality. However, you must focus first on your thoughts and claim possession, and you will have it very soon. Yes, you can dream it, you can have it. However, your vibrational thoughts must follow by the actual action, and this momentum transforms into reality and becomes your final destination.

• You must be passionate about what you do—Your pleasing personality will guide you to meet many people who would like to work with you.

• You must be able to control yourself—You must know yourself and acknowledge your inner world to help you carry out your wishes. You become the master of your own destiny.

• You go the extra mile for the things that you do—Your willingness to do more than you are paid for in your job. You don't mind doing extra work for others, without getting paid.

• You must be able to distinguish the truth—Your ability to separate fact from fabrication.

• You must pay attention to what is surrounding you—You must keep focused on your plans until you are certain of your decision and then it will emerge to meet your intention to create a better environment.

• Synchronicities of events that can bring you success—Synchronicity are significant events that happen for various reasons and the internal and external factors may not be the causes related to this. It happens for a short period of time, the people, the places and the circumstances will leave you after this interval period. These events must happen for you to experience both spiritual growth and influence in your life, because it has already happened in the fifth dimension before it occurred in the third dimension here. It is related to you and the possible influence of attracting the ultimate success in your life.

• You learn by your failure—You learn to appreciate your failures and give you a chance to improve and learn from your mistake. You are aware that your failures are only temporary and you have faith and belief, that you will reverse these mistakes. Once we realize the problem then the "worst" scenario is you learn from those experiences. As soon as we recognize them, the whole dilemma fades and a new portal opens to us, and new possibilities have always been there, only when we look in the right direction. That's the real power that overrides our failures and helps us to realize our ultimate fulfillment, happiness, and success.

• Practice forgiveness—You must learn to forgive others that have hurt you in the past. Forgiveness opens the door of opportunities. Hate and intolerance closes the door of importance. It will only confuse the mind to create many doubts and prejudices.

• Trust your Inner Source to sustain you—Always follow and listen to your heart's guide to do the right thing. Your Inner Source is the only source you can trust and relate to and use that innate desire to help yourself and others.

• Hints and Support—Often times, we look inside for support, but forget about the external world around us— there are people and resources looking for you that can lead you to the open door and assist you through to inspire action. (This hints and clues are in fact sent from **The Source** to help you and you must not defy them.)

• Universal consciousness—Get connected with the world through one single mind to create "win," "win" situations. Attracting the right people and to create your desire almost instantaneously and getting the result you desire. It is because, the human minds can trigger an illumination, and able to

connect with other human minds. This charged energy creates
a harmonious vibration, which brings a tranquil and an
effective tool to amend your thoughts to improve your life.

Success is power in the mind and its thoughts. It can't be equally
positive or negative at the same time. One will dominate the other. Since
the mind reflects our habitual thoughts therefore, it is our responsibilities
to influence our mind with positive energy. Success is the evolution of
vibrational thought, which connects with the Universal Mind to assist a
person who wishes to succeed in life. In order to connect to the power
of success a person must realize the potential of the power of his mind.
He must utilize the *Law of Magnetic Energy* to use this powerful tool and
can be easily applied.

It becomes noticeable, when one learns this special technique of
tuning into the source of this power and his outer environment. This
technique is learned through the *Universal Collective Consciousness* and a
person does not need to be in the same location to gain this knowledge.
This technique is even more powerful than millions of computers
linked together to form a huge network across the globe. The
consciousness thoughts are more powerful than the global computers
network. The consciousness power can connect to any *Higher Infinite
Conscious* soul remotely without knowing each other, but able to connect.
It is through this innate power of your thought energy that effectively
connects us to other consciousness souls with the same intention, which
shifts our consciousness to receive the real data between our
subconscious mind and the *Universal Mind.* The connection forms a huge
powerful net and gains a collective knowledge to influence the levels of
awareness and pursue the truth in life. Only by careful analysis, extended
practice and an open mindedness do you discover yourselves if this is
a truth.
If one tiny portion of the right brain is used to store collective
information and the mind can be triggered to connect and interact with
other minds and the *Universal Life Force.* Imagine you can use the infinite

36

power you already have and the technique to influence your world by controlling your thoughts and shape your life.

This is not imagination, but is a fact that you can create the kind of life you have always wanted through the power of your positive thoughts and aligned with the *Universal Mind*, which brings your desire from perfect health to obtaining wealth and that is a part of your life's greater plan and the door is open for you and you will never fail.

The power of vibration is a form of energy, which brings everything into action. Sound wave is produced through vibration.

In fact, everything in this *Universe* and on the planet Earth is manifested through vibration. It is possible that vibration energy causes us to think in a precise way and this precious gift is from **The Source**.

A typical example of a sound rhythm is created through vibration, when you place a number of guitars together as soon as you touch one string it affects the other to vibrate a sound rate. The power of intervening vibrations affects the other guitars and reverberated with each other in harmony to cause them to vibrate in the same rhythm. However, we have to pay attention to the gap to realize the effect of the vibrations on the guitars, because we may not hear, see, or feel the movement as the guitar does.

Where is this gap and how do you enter into this empty place to obtain what you desire? The emptiness is a beautiful space! It is a different dimension where miracles happen. It is this space between the gap and the silence. You and everyone can enter into this empty gap. It is a peaceful and tranquil place where you can make a conscious connection with **The Source**.

In fact, you can enter into this empty place through meditation at any time and there is no restriction to how many times you can tap into this beautiful space called the "*silence*."

You have learned to enter into the empty space called the "*silence*" and make conscious contact with **The Source**. You want to succeed in your business venture, in your family life or a particular career you want to enter into, and then you practice medication to enter the "*silence*."

Through the power of meditation, your mind is motionless and enters into the deeper alpha stage of inner silence, where God's dwells. It is the sacred place you can talk to God in silence and seek *His* guidance and direction. You can express your concern about your needs, difficulties, and despairs in your daily activities. It is also a place where you can seek to heal, create, and often a vision will occur at this level of silence through the access of meditation and of course, at the same time you seek to generate a union with **The Source.**

Meditating is a path to clear all your clutter in your conscious mind and enter below that cluttered surface. You need to navigate below that noise plane. You dive into the deep and feel the tranquility and peace. Then, many positive vibrational thoughts come to you and open your senses. Suddenly, an idea aligns in your mind's eye; you have visualized a clear image that you are sitting in a huge conference room and windows connected to the floor. You glance outside and there is this tremendous view of the whole Greater Vancouver, and you are there to negotiate a contract with a major client and finally reach the consensus and signing the accord with them. A month later you are actually in the conference room you had perceived earlier and sign an important contract, which is exactly as you perceived it. It is precisely in that gap a profound transformation has taken place, the miracle was created, and the infinite possibilities await you.

You know that your thoughts are manifested through vibration and able to consciously connected with many other minds.

Some people are capable of sending brain waves and the vast of series of vibrations into someone's mind to interrupt them. This brain wave could be sent from anywhere flowing through time-space remotely and setting a thought in them, in other words, each human mind can receive and broadcast this energy to influence the vibrations of their thoughts. This is because of the power of thoughts in the mind.

You can dream big and think big. The *Law of Abundance* states that you will receive what you are seeking and will visually be manifested at your command and does come from your spiritual connection. All you

THE SPIRITUAL MEDICINE - THE POWER OF SUCCESS

have to do is be in alignment with **The Source** and consider it is done and you will get it soon. In short, whatever we consciously think about and we will receive. Because, thought is energy and energy is power. It is the energy vibrating through you travelling to the empty space, hanging there for some time and meeting with other consciousness with the same idea and releasing this creative thought, which vibrate and eventually become mature, and because energy sent out must bounce back to the sender in the physical world and consequently, becomes your own reality.

When you send out your request to receive abundance in your life and you may not receive it instantly. Because, a certain requirement is needed to be met, before you will receive what you are asking for. What happens is this, after you have manifested your thought energies to the *Universe* for financial abundance, do you still have old negative thoughts in you that prevent you from receiving what you desire. You must feel content. Your emotions will show whether you are near or far away from it.

Do you feel vibration harmony with your *Source?* You need to affirm what you ask for and you hold your intentions to attract financial abundance and success into your life, because that is who you are. Your goal is to eliminate any distance between your objective of what you desire and the obtaining your accomplishment. Success is not out there waiting for you to show up, but believe that you have already received it.

Do not be afraid to ask for a big desire, because it does not have an effect on what you receive. You must keep yourself in the higher frequency to sustain the vibrational harmony with **The Source**. Remember the *Universe* has unlimited supply and there is always enough for you and everyone, and there is no scarcity, but only abundance and the *Universe* is willing to help you to succeed.

You have manifested your wish into action and imagine seeing the end with thrive results. For example, if it is the business you want to sell, then you must put your conscious mind into action, talk with people with confidence; make marketing phone calls and networking with other business acquaintances to increase your chances of success. Do everything with passion and enthusiasm and pay attention to details and hints that guide you to places, circumstance and people you meet and anything that seems to indicate you are predestined to be there. Monitor your emotional feelings that you are in alignment with your *Inner Knowing* to activate the power of the *Universal Creative Life Force* to work for you. You have the whole Universal force to support you.

You can't fail, but gain success. You're feeling positive that you are near the mountain peak of where you opt to be and meditate to perceive the final destination and gain the success end results.

After, you have gained success and abundance in your life. You need to show gratitude to the *Universe* and to share your wealth with others. It will be a joyful experiences and your willingness to share fortune with others and let others celebrate the joy and bliss of your success.

Because by broadening your abundant energy and generously share with others and keep the flow by not owning it and free yourself from worldly attachments, will move you to stay in alignment, which brings about the vibrational harmony with **The Source**.

Finally, you must know genuine success is the awareness of your conscious thoughts, and are responsive to your own power and centering yourself to meditate on **The Source** to obtain peace and blissful state of the mind. There is no other alternatives that can bring you desire, but through the omnipotence and omnipresence of **The Source**. Because, when you are in alignment with **The Source**, immediately you feel the peace and everything is possible and promising. Since everything is possible through the connection with your *Source*, then there is nothing omitted, consequently fears and worries have no influence in your thoughts. Remember everything happened for a reason and everything has happened for the best and if nothing happens, that is not the end. You must continue to be grateful of what you already have and feel happy. You are your own source and for everything else you have the whole *Universe* within you, behind you, above and below and also the external world support you.

In conclusion, everything happened has a Divine purpose and scarcity is only an illusion and because by providing more services to others and you will notice more increasing returns. Failure will teach you lessons that will show you that you can gain experience and have success waiting for you.

Chapter Two
~Your Life Purpose—What Do You Want in Your Life~

Everything on this planet Earth has its limits in life and there are no exceptions to this principal of Universal laws of existence. There are limitations because in the physical world our powers are limited to physical resource and are due to the configuration and the structure of our existences. However, this limitation is not only applied to all living organisms, but also applies to equipment you have in possession now. Nevertheless, the good news is human power is unlimited in the infinite world. You can have anything you desire, to do and to be with your infinite power.

Your Infinite power is **The Source** dwelling from within. Your *Inner Knowing* is the most powerful source that is consciously connects with the *Mind of God*. You can use this Infinite power of thoughts and the power of creative visualization to create a virtual image by focusing it in the mind's eye and hold this image and transform this thought energy into form and returns to the physical world, and becomes your own reality. It is the power of your thoughts, which brings about the vibration harmony that you are co-operating with the *Mind of God* and the power of intention to know that you will receive all that is created because it is the link to your heart's desire.

When you are called upon by a great purpose, your inspiration is ignited by the passion in your heart that creates the need and joys in your life. Everything will work out great for you. This inspiration is supported by spirit and therefore nothing can go wrong with your intention and follow the path that urges you on. There is no risk because you follow your bliss, which is **The Source** within you.

This is only love working in harmony with your true intention. This is the truth from within, if you don't feel love, you don't feel the truth and connection to your spirit. That is why inspiration becomes the most important part of a fulfillment of your intention and leads awakening to your purpose in life.

The reason why you have emerged here is not an accident, but there is a reason and a purpose waiting for you in your life journey. The *Invisible Creative Life Force* of the *Universal Mind* is responsible for all existence here. You must know what you are doing. You are part of a creation and your infinite mind is connected to it. There's always meaning to your existence and you have the capacity to live life from the condition set out by love.

The purpose of you being here is to use your inner abilities to discover the life you want to pursue and what to expect in the future. You can always count on God leads you out into the open, into a free auspicious life.

As you move towards your spiritual journey I know it is not easy, it holds a deep secret that once you realize this it will transform your life forever. You will in your own journey open yourself to see the truth from within. Once you're determined to see your purpose, you then follow your desire and to continue to evolve until you reach your destination. If your intention is moving in the direction of spirituality, then God will do his duty to assist you towards your desire.

In the beginning, you may find your spiritual journey is full of thorns, difficulties and confusions, but you can transcend them into triumph by affirming your intention and having faith in yourself and your *Source* to keep you focused and to grow towards what you want to see manifested in your life and all things come from the power of love.

The way to establish a relationship with God and access the power of this creative principle is to continue to meditate in silence as being surrounded by the condition you wish to produce. You must trust and believe that God's infinite power will produce the result your desire. This creating power is the creating force of the *Universe*. As your spiritual life grows deeper through your meditation and prayer, you will find everything is from within and you have God's power to create anything you want and ultimately, fulfill your heart's dearest desire.

Changes start with an idea. To live a spiritual life it helps to focus on your intention. Its aim is to create freedom and limitless possibilities. The world is united in one and you are an infinite being with God. You are conscious of caring for yourself and as well as working toward God's purpose in promoting health, prosperity, positive relationships leading to happiness and intrinsic harmony.

Since, you cannot predict the future, but you can depend on your *Divine* for guidance through prayer, meditation, contemplation, and vibration. Through Ascended Masters, enlightenment, sage, Saints, deities and the like, these are the ways of contacting **The Source**. Dedication and devotion to spirituality is a perquisite for success.

If there is one reality, nothing in the material world prevents you from getting it; God. All you need to do is decide, which part you do and God will dedicate *His*. It will also change circumstances and you must be aware of yourself in this regard. Your intention is the most powerful device at your own disposal. Intention will generate results, as it should, then let go and see if clues approach your way. However, pay attention to the *Inner Voice* speaking to you and guides you naturally, and you must let go of any doubt and trusting **The Source** to lead you to your destination.

You can enjoy God more by devoting part of your life to worship *Him*, love *Him* and know about *Him* and gradually you could be the most enlighten person in the *Universe*—keep in mind always surrender to the *Divine Light* regularly. You will begin fulfill the glory of God and your purpose on Earth.

The part of you already knows you do not need to search and it will surface soon. And when you implement new desires, an uplifting ideas, or a profound thought or insights you have created and activated the energy to transcend into the *Unknown* from the physical world and will translate your individual mental picture into physical form. The *Unknown* is the sacred place and know the power of your *Source* cares about the fate of your spirit; therefore, it is good to admire this, as much as you admire holiness. As God holiness lives in the *Unknown*, and when you can embrace it fully then you will be home free.

Some people view life like a movie, a circus, a minefield, and a journey, but it mirrors what we believe. How we will act in the movie depends on how we will view ourselves in the real world. Sometimes you feel the life of ups and downs or it keeps going around and around in circles with no direction. Occasionally, if you play a game of cards you have to play it right. You have to play the hand you are dealt. Our future is in flux. But, you can trust God to take care of everything. You can enjoy everything without even need to possess.

What is our life propose. Why are we here? That is what we are here to find out. Our life purposes are to find out who we are. We have to begin with lessons in learning to enhance our spiritual life. We have to learn how to face challenges and events in life. We are learning to recall who we really are in reality. You may view your life challenge based on the purpose of God set for you by meditate within and then you will know God and realize the omnipresence of God.

In a spiritual view of life, we are here to learn different forms of lessons. You were born into different circumstances whether pleasant or unpleasant, you have to go through these assignments that are necessary for your advancement. Do not judge. Listen to your *Inner Voice*. Have faith and trust in *Him*. The real self is reflected from the inner state of mind, which loves and benefits all.

We should feel God's peace. With God's peace, we have bliss and joy. We surrender ourselves to circumstances that we have no control and handle the situation in a calm and peaceful way. In this way, you can think clearly, the solution will come to you from within, without panic.

Every creation has a solution and yet every problem has an exit. It works well in a relationship and circumstances. If you are involved in an argument with your partner or someone close to you, begin observing, how the situation could change to benefit both parties. Then, suddenly you realize that you have a choice, you may decide to drop your own reaction and surrender to love.

Your mind controls your subconscious thought. Your mind creates your reality. You can do anything, if you let your mind lead you. If you defy the power of the *Inner Mind*, it will prevent your ability to achieve your aims. Remember we have power. What you sow is what you reap. You control your destiny through the power within. What is reflected on the glass of your memories and thoughts is mirrored back to you.

Your mind is a powerful instrument. It is there to assist you with your specific task and when the task is done, you put it away. Your mind can also bring you many negative thoughts and sometimes harmful action so train your mind and use it wisely.

Your real self is reflected from your inner state to the external consciousness. By practicing yoga daily, you improve your connection with the *Divine*. It will change your vision of how you perceive life. You become more attentive, as your focus grows. Your inner world gives you the wisdom, knowledge, and aptitude to know what to do, along with the power to achieve your goals.

A lotus flower may live in the center of a muddy pond; this beautiful flower stands above the mud and remains clean and pure and you live a quality spiritual life. Lucid your thoughts and prevent it from creating harm to others, because your thoughts have power.

If you want to live a spirit-enriching life, you must change your inner state of consciousness, so that the view of your external world is in alignment with **The Source**. For it to be balanced together you must take responsibility for your life. Your thoughts and actions must be the same. You may have to go through difficult events and tasks before you reach your triumph. Your goal can be attained, but you need to summon the right elements to assist you.

(For example, eliminate your pride, and maintain positive thoughts, attitude and actions, you must have faith to control unnecessary emotions, and trust your inner guides. In life, we experience many difficulties and perplexed situation our tasks is to overcome them with the help of our Inner Wisdom we can solve it.)

However, we can also use our inner talent to help each other life; we can also transform our lives through compassion and empathy. You have empathy towards others, because of your personal experience. You can feel other pains, because you have been there and that transmutes your perception about life. Empathy expands to all living organisms in the *Universe*. In other words, we are all one with God. You share other joys and pains and realize that their compassions are your love for yourself.

Your sympathy will increase when you eliminate all angers, hatred, greed, envy and release your suppressions from within. You then become more attentive to your thoughts and intentions. You have a different way of responding and perceiving the world.

You desire to live an abundant and successful life thus you need to surrender yourself to the *Universal Source*. Surrender does not denote that you need to renounce everything, but you simply let the invisible power guide you to do what is appropriate for you. (For example, *due to mental resistant you unknowingly separate yourself from the material world. You subconsciously manifested a portal of inner mental emotional state, which prevented you from associate with others besides your family. It is a mental state created in your subconscious mind without you being aware of it. You have let your ego take control of your thoughts and emotional consciousness.*

An ego is a false mind. Gradually, you follow whatever the ego tells you to do and separating yourself from others and cease all communications except within your own inner world. Eventually, you became very isolated and it strengthens the feeling of separateness on which the ego depends on its survival. As its condition grows, you cannot get out. The portal is closed; you are now being cut off from the inner dimension, the dimension of state of being alone. As you surrender, your condition softens and become somewhat transparent, as it were, so the un-manifest can shine on you. It is up to you to open a portal in your life and give your consciousness access to the un-

manifested. Stay awake, get in touch with your inner state of mind, and surrender to what is.)

There are portals you can use, however, surrender to the one you need the most that can help you to enhance in your life. Surrender to God means giving your trust and faith to *Him*. You can fall back fully, and have faith and belief that God will catch you. Faith is complete trust in *Him*.

Trust eliminates doubt, allowing a miracle to take place. Prayer is the medium of miracles. We simply have to trust and believe even if your prayer is unanswered. God will watch your response to unanswered prayers, your faith, and problems. God tests you on what is really in your heart and prepare you for a greater transformation, and reveal a weakness and prepare you for more responsibility.

When you understand life is a lesson, you realize nothing is really missing in your life. Every lesson is important and has significance in your character to development. You can depend on God to deepen your character, develop your love, or to depend on *Him* entirely. He will never put you in a situation you can't handle. You are always in good hands, when you acknowledge *His* will. Every time you complete a lesson, God will notice it and will reward you in eternity.

Perhaps you will ask what your life's challenge is. It could be accepting success, wealth, fame, survival, caring, protection, helping others and family and surrendering to God. Once you have faced enough challenges in your life and you will set your goals even higher, such as, humanity works.

You would like to lend your heart and mind to help others. You are more conscious of what you do. You start to feel empathy towards others and offer your generous help and love to them. You meditate on compassion in your heart to help others. You spend more time with others, rather than your own needs. You are an advocate in dealing with others and that is your priority.

What's your greatest strength? What should you do to survive in a harsh world—you have to show courage in the face of difficulties.

You need to keep a conscious mind on love and empathy so that you can eliminate negative emotions and accept your true being. Do not let fear overpower you and to overcome this hurdle. Do not let fear imprison you. (*For example, keeping quiet in a circumstance will only make thing worse, since it has no solution. You need to face the troubles.*) You need to show the person "I am not afraid of you." Then, you will move to a higher stage of no fear and win the battle of fearlessness. Believe that God is around you and *He* will not allow any human souls to hurt you. You can accept and trust God to protect you, to sustain you, bless you in all circumstances, in time of danger and turmoil. He lifts you from any adverse events and removes you from danger so that you are free from harm.

What's your greatest temptation? The greatest temptation may be to overthrow a tyrant even though it might be wrong or inappropriate. It happens when a country is ruled by a tyranny. People cannot tolerate this anymore and are tempted to overthrow the dictator by force. People smoking illegal drugs are tempted by invisible force. Therefore, they become disobedient. They were frightened by outside influence and they become fearful. They need a protector to protect them.

You must open yourself to find your purpose. Your thoughts become your words. Every decision you make is also a part of you. It reflects who you are and whether you are a thoughtful or thoughtless person. How you dress, what you wear and what color you like.

What part of the *Universe* do you come from? Now your home also reflects the nature of your inner world. That also affects your identity. You must be aware life is changing all the time? It changes constantly and makes rooms for new challenge. Each level has different scenario, and lesson to learn and recognize that these events occur randomly, but you must undo this rope and God will give you the strength to endure it so that you will find an exit.

At different stages, we experience different needs. When you reach the highest level in the physical world, your need is transforming.

Material stuff is not your priority. You are not looking for wealth and power. You have achieved it all. You may want to do things differently to meet your inner needs.

You understand money and wealth is only temporary. You don't own it, but you respect and acknowledge the trust of God. All things come from God and He is entrusting you to look after earthly things and you must show you are worth that trust. Then, God will evaluate the situations and reward you accordingly.

You may start to see and feel the pain of people. You are a giver. You begin to seek for your spiritual realities. Your benevolence comes out. You become more spiritually engage and begin charitable works, because of the urging of your benevolent self. You like to give back what you have gained from the community. That is the nature reflected in you.

You simply, wait for events to occur and your patience with your infinite self helps to transform thoughts of empathy through to the *Universe* and become the reality of your desires.

If you pay attention, you know what you want from the material world. Observe now, what are you doing, pay attention to details, and the environment around you, and you will find the truth in you. After all, in this life, our action speaks for all of us.

Do you really know who you are? Do you have choices when you come to this life; do you choose to be western instead of eastern, do you choose your body and your final destination?

Your destiny was written before you entered a body. However, as soon as you leave your body, your soul flows freely to the *Universe*, until you are connected to a new home. It is a tree of life.

Like a pigeon resting on the branch, can fly away. Your choices will dissolve in the wind once you leave this body. It does not matter what life you live. When you leave your body, your soul will find a new body and a new you.

When you pass on, your soul floats above your body, then you realize you are a spiritual being. You then know who you are.

Do you accept your destiny?

Illness is part of our karma, and is important for people to experience their own cause and effect, associated with their personal beliefs or disbelief about life and the surrounding *Universe*. If you could see beyond the illusion realm of subjective experience, your body is suffering, but you are not.

Certainly good karma will be replaced the old karma. The same will apply, if you do something wrong, you probably will expect rocky returns.

Instead you pray for everybody during your silent connection with the *Divine*, you have created a bond with yourself and your world, but this also transform your good energy to everyone and it benefits the whole *Universe*, overtime you will feel a big change around you.

Somewhere along the road of life, you may be betrayed by people you trust. Someone may even break her words or your heart. You may feel resentment for the pain caused by their lack of consideration or harmful action.

You are still feeling the resentment of pain for a while, and then you come to realize that there is no reason to be angry or resentful towards anyone, at least not in extended periods, because you know that resentment dampens the light of your own happiness. You simply give your power away and you hurt yourself.

If someone does not help you when you are in need, do not feel bad or resentful about it. Instead, you should work through it. Use it as an experience to increase your own sense of compassion. Use that experience to promise yourself to be more aware and open to helping others in need. True forgiveness lifts you up to a higher level of consciousness into a more extended field of perception and profound view of life.

You need to forgive yourself probably at some point, consciously or unconsciously for the harm that you caused to others with or without your intention. You can ask for forgiveness from yourself or from the *Divine*. You can also ask for forgiveness from someone you have harmed in person or in your heart. Maintaining the spiritual awareness of God's presence will allow all your virtues to unfold naturally.

You need to move beyond forgiveness, if you forgive someone, then you no longer judge or are harbor him/her, but you should not hide some resentment inside yourself. A true forgiveness is to rise to a wider view of life and have faith that everything happens for a reason and everything ultimately happens for the best, and believe everything that happens is God's will. Once you see a clear picture of the person you are forgiving, you are only acting out God's will and your own destiny. Ultimately, there is no blame, or personal responsibility, which is separate from the will of the *Divine* force, which creates, sustains, and forever shifts each individual atom object and activity in this *Universe*.

When an upsetting incident happens, you may feel rushed, frustrated, or angry. It is normal and is a part of the experience you are meant to have in this situation. Nevertheless, with higher spiritual awareness you quickly are able to put things in a proper prospective and rise back into a peaceful state of mind. You will probably notice when you get angry, your anger will not last long, because you center yourself to your higher spiritual identity.

You choose your destiny and it is not who you are or what your life is like. Your soul urges you to be the best at everything that you do. You can be directly connected to a higher power and be grateful of what you have. Gratitude is the magic formula, not only for forgiveness, but also for happiness and peacefulness, along with worldly and spiritual success.

When you are grateful, you are likely to be in a better mood, friendlier and generous toward others. This kind of gratefulness creates a better life and makes you into a better person, who works well with others, and relates to others with kindness and love.

On a spiritual level, it helps to draw to you a shining light, while others can come to help you. Your thoughts and feeling are flowing through to the *Universe* and return to you with a fabulous result. The world is as you see it!

Life is like a mirror it reflects your reality. Every time you transform the way you vision your life, the *Universe* will reflect your new outlook of truth. However, it may not occur instantly, because of circumstances may not allow it to manifest immediately. You decide what your intention are and make changes, and you are encircled by this magnetic potential, as it influences your circumstances to adapt into a new form where the new reality will be able to manifest and operate.

Reflection will soon fabricate your manifestation. But if you do not like your life, attempt to discover a way to generate a right reflection and you will transform your inner vision in order to change the view and you will receive it from the *Universe*. The mirror of life will reflect happiness inside you, if you decide to do so; your inner state will reflect a happy person. Afterward, it will reflect your new reality.

Your intentions hold knowledge, of what you are, doing. To do so you must tap into your sub-conscious perception of truth in reality. You think of what you would like to explore in life. You write a list of ideas, which you would like to accomplish. Think of each idea and see which one is closer to your heart desires. You then determine what you want to explore.

You may realize that all you want is to live with the flow of life and be happy. This *Universe* is ready to live through your subconscious mind to bring you your desire, and success. Give and you shall receive and the more you give away, the more affluence will return to you. Utilize your subconscious mind to develop your communication and agreement with the *Universal Force* is the key to personal power. In addition, you need to make your intentions known and surrender to follow your heart to hear the *Divine* love's communication and connect to *His* abundance and light.

Often, you are on the defensive side of your negative feelings. You make excuses or deny an incident, which is not your fault. You just cannot accept the reality from right to wrong. You are merely hiding your real self from the world. We tend to neglect one side or the other and it is our nature. Typically, it is our shortcomings. Perhaps you feel your action is justified "*under the circumstances.*"

As a result, only one part of you is responding, it causes a great depletion in your life. Thus, it would be better to admit the mistake than defending it. Therefore, a holistic approach is appropriate to balancing the creative energy according to what is needed or desired.

(For example, a drain problem in your kitchen may be small, however if you do not look after it and call a plumber in to resolve the problem. Eventually, it will cause you more than you can imagine. In other words, problem is too small, why bother solving it, is a wrong idea. Simply, trust your logic and you are free from this problem in the future and this is worth the little effort today, and do what you can to plug that niggling leak).

Where there is an ego, there is no love. On the contrary, "*selfless is love.*" Ego has no love. Think about any negative emotion—envy, hatred, avarice, rage—these are the fruits of ego. Its roots are "*I*" and "*mine.*" But, love is the most powerful destroyer of the ego.

If you trust and have faith in God, you will feel transformed and enlighten in your life. The ego, by nature, will adopt any identity, but love. The ego is only concern about being in the center of the *Universe* and is associated with the ego centeredness.

The ego is "*I*" and "*mine.*" The ego is only concerned with what is in it for him. It is doing either his way or the highway. The ego also dwells in you, if you let it control your mind. You will be negative about things, except for love.

The ego is the negative force in you while love is God in you. While, there is an ego there cannot be any love and where there is selfless love, there is the light force.

Success could be obtained in many different ways. Having a full life is also successful. Success does not mean having tons of funds in the bank. (It won't hurt you to have it in the material world) You reach a feeling in your internal condition of consciousness a reflection that shows your bliss and joy to you.

The Past is history, the future is a flux, and the present is…a gift. One of the major reasons why you fail to find happiness or to establish a unique lifestyle is because you have not yet manage the art of living. The art of living is learning to dwell in the present, which is "*Now*." It is the *Now*, which you relate to and draws the wealth of experience and joy to you. The way to live is capturing every moment, and becomes a new part of who you are and what you will be. The way of life is not what you do, but how you experience and relate to it.

And until you learn to live in the now, you may not master the lifestyle you were indented to have. Your life style improves through your connection to spiritual life and uplifts your relationship with family, and your health. It forms a unique lifestyle, which you create to fit your distinctive personality and forms the life that you wish to proceed with.

The healthy lifestyle could be obtained in many ways:
- Spending time with nature
- Doing exercise has also been shown to keep your mind sharp and improve mental health, and help avoid depression, live at peace and live longer.
- Keep your minds active.
- Provide a service to others.
- Keep a healthy diet and quit all bad habits.
- Fill your environment or your home with happy decoration, such as pictures and objects.
- Doing meditation—alert and spacious calm of your mind
- Assign time with God and feel God's peace within you
- The most important person is the one you are within that moment
- Spend time in silence and feel the blissful and peace from within

For your dream and desire to come alive, you need the support of invisible factor at work. You may call this heaven, earth, man and the environmental luck or even just the invisible blessings from Heaven.

When compared to these essences, it is not great wealth or even born with a silver spoon that is important if one of these important factors is missing. These four essences of blessings must be present to gain success and wealth. Heaven's luck is connected with the *Divine* from within. Earth luck is the five elements, which are air, water, and fire, wood and metal to bring you the energy in order to achieve special desired results. Human luck is when; helpful people emerge synchronically in your life to assist your growth and development. Environment luck is when *Universal's Sources* energy that connects you with the appropriate environment or geographical region. (You are emerging at the right time and in the right place and to be offered your dream desires.) This real significance enhances and embraces your power to success and abundance. These four essences are alive and very real.

The greatest joy in life is to discover what your life journey on earth is and your life's direction, you made many decisions, but there is only one decision that matters, and the answer to that decision, is from *within*. Once you discover what your life purpose is, then your life will be transformed to a new level. The new level, which will enrich your soul and continue creating and expanding your well-being, as you continue to grow and explore your soul-journey on earth.

Now you are ready to make new changes, you understand life on Earth is only temporary and prepare you to live for eternity. The soul is the immortal nature of an individual life. According to the basic principles of spirituality, you are here to experience life on earth as a unique infinite being.

It is true that you are here for a reason and you have a sole purpose and are preparing for something even better. You are here to experience and challenge the discontent and dissatisfaction in life this will develop you spiritually and prepare you for infinity. Yet, your unique personality and character will also be tested. You therefore, have a sole purpose within the multi-dimension of creation.

You understand you were born to an environment whether it is pleasant or unpleasant you have to accept it. It is because you are here to reflect life on Earth and take on this test before you progress to the next level. These are the tests, which challenges your *Higher Inner Self* respond to your current life. However, it is not a judgment kind of test; it simply helps you so that you can progress to the next lesson.

There is no pass or failure in this evaluation test; it simply helps you to comprehend the Universal laws and your learning on Earth. Most importantly, it works with your inner transformation and grows with the experience by going through it.

As soon as you walked through each challenge made available to you. You have learned a lot about the Divine's character just by looking around and followed the flow of your life, you begin to understand through nature knowing God is powerful, even though you have experienced many difficulties and perplexities, you know God will sustain you and reveal *His* love to you and guide you out of the turmoil.

In conclusion, the purpose in life is you were born to learn the purpose God has for you. It is God who directs and delivers *His* purpose and all life is within *His* power and love. You must begin with God and *His* word, your creator. It is through God we discover our origin, our intention, our significance, and our destiny. Life is about letting God use you for *His* purpose.

Pay attention to God lead us to abundance and success, into auspicious free life. You become what God created to be. God will fulfill *His* purpose for you. God left no details to chance, but He planned it all for *His* purpose. Therefore, nothing in your life is surprise. It's all happens for a reason. So, regardless of your circumstance at your birth, you can celebrate the fact that God created you to be just "*you*."

Chapter Three
~Your Self-Respect—No One Can Give You That Respect but Yourself~

The ego is the absence of true knowledge of who you really are, along with its result: a fate holding on to something at all costs and feeling temporarily disconnected with the union of self and the mind, an inevitably misrepresentation of yourself image continues changing, because it must keep itself alive about its existence.

You are part of a whole '*Universe*,' a place limited in time and space. You experience self, your thoughts, and feelings that seem to be separated from the rest—a kind of optical illusion of your perceptional awareness. This illusion is restricting our connection and our affection for other people closer to us. Our task must be to free ourselves of this limitation by widening our circles of compassion to embrace all living creatures and the physical world and its beauty.

Two little people dwell within your heart. One is very talkative, demanding, hysterical, mean, and calculating. While the silent one is the hidden infinite being, and a little quiet voice of wisdom you have seldom heard. As you listen to your *Inner Voice*, it enhances your *Inner Wisdom* of judgment and is known as "*discriminating awareness*."

Once you have heard this awareness, it is awakened and you are empowered by this experience of enlightenment, which has separated you from the enchanting voice of the ego. The memory of your real natural self, with all its magnificence and confidence, begins to return to you.

The only person that respects you is yourself and no one can give you that experience. In your own creative experience, you have your own uniqueness and ability to create anything you want in life. Since you and **The**

Source are not separated, but united therefore, when you love and trust **The Source** that created you, means you will have respect and confidence in yourself. On the contrary, when you fail to love and trust yourself, you become misaligned with your *Source*. Your feelings become very wavering and unsteady. You attract things that are unintended, which brings about disharmony and painful experiences into your current life. You have no known idea, how this enters into your experience. This is because you have denied your *Source* and in favor of the ego. You have your own choice to either be a host of **The Source** or being a prisoner to your ego.

Your ego will tear you down and destroy the ways and means in your life if you invite and allow it to do so. Your emotional disruption affects your self-respect and your alliance to your true self. Your moods become wavering and very unsteady because of lower self-esteem. Your ego is solely responsible for your lower self-esteem and you may be unaware of this dwelling in the lower vibration energy field.

When you are dwelling in the lower energy field with ego-center controlling your life, you are a prisoner to its unworthiness. Your worth as a person is always measured by the acquisitions, net-worth, and accomplishments. You feel insecure if you have fewer possessions, and are feeling invaluable and therefore less respected by peers and not able to compete with rivals. If others don't respect you, it is because you are holding on to sacristy and the belief you have no power to change yourself. You drag yourself down, because you under estimate yourself and others. These emotions are only an illusion created by your ego to hurt and confuse you. It will continue to become your own truth and reality if you allow it.

Your ego believes you are living in scarcity, separated from everyone and especially **The Source** in your life, feeling further abandon and lacking trust and believing yourself. If you are controlled by your ego's system, then you are always in competition with others even if there is no apparent reason for this. The ego will not allow you to think positive or to see what is real and let go of the illusion.

You are in the state of denial and are deceive. The ego will always make sure you are the prisoner and never allow you to be the host to love and have control of your own life.

However, being the host to your *Source* is always being yourself and have the authentic power to control your environment and most importantly, keeping your connection to **The Source** demonstrate you have empowered yourself and alleviate the problems of the ego's doing.

You must always believe you are worth of receiving love, health, wealth, and success into your life. You must allow higher energy to flow to you. The closer you are to this energy, the more aligned you are to **The Source**. It means the possibilities of what you have just created and transformed into reality is near. All because you respect yourself and this allows your intention to be fully fulfilled and realized.

The *Law of Magnetic Energy* will support and sustain all your beliefs in abundance, when you affirm your worth and acknowledge **The Source** for its response. You are sending a message to the *Universe* that you are content and allow the flow of your desire emerge to you, because you have trusted you are worthy of receiving it. The *Universe* will start sending you what is requested by you and you will probably receive more than you can imagine.

What you perceive inside is what you have projected to the external world. Your internal state of mind reflects how happy and how sad you are in that present moment. If your internal consciousness is in vibrational harmony with your emotions, you are connected to the moment. However, when you are feeling disharmony and misalignment with your *Source*, you are sadden and disinterested in anything that is presented to you. Every window, door, portal, and opportunity is closed and all connections are lost. All of these attitudes are your own wrongful assessment and your interaction with life.

If these reassessments are true, then they reflect the thought in your mind, and that's how you feel about your life. Whatever attitude you carry, you then see the external world indicating the respect of your abilities and what you intend to do in this world.

Regardless of what others might think. You have determined that you and your *Source* are always connected. In this way, you respect your *Higher Source* that has created you. You declare all your achievements, glories and acquisitions are coming from **The Source**. You accept who you are and can't change what God had created; you are perfect. You have an intended purpose on Earth. You can begin by fulfill this intention to live a life of self-respect by honoring this body, which is the host for your *Infinite Soul*. You know what to do by logging in, listen to your inner wisdom and lov'ing it.

You should not allow others to make you feel inferior or be offended by someone so easily. At any time, you should remind yourself do not compare yourself to anyone, because it will create uncomfortable feelings and could cause hatred and envy ultimately misalignment from **The Source**.

However, if this happens immediate you recharge this thought and realign your thoughts and ideas related to **The Source** and direct and monitor your thoughts to observe yourself, and resolve the situation so that it becomes capable of creative thought and the ability to keep focus on the word of truth and God's love.

You are not separate from **The Source**. With the self as a focal point, you have the illusion that you are actually separated from everybody especially **The Source**. With the self-importance, it is difficult to carry out your true intention. You are a spiritual being but with the body. The body is the host to your spirit. Eliminate the ego concept of self-importance and you have identified with your true self. The most important thing is you are connected with **The Source** and carry out your real intention on Earth.

You must not let other disrespect words intimidated you. Because, you can't be offended unless you allow them to enter your comfort zone and disturb God's peace in you. The simple explanation is when you feel you are being attacked this leads to counter-attack and the creation of negative destructive energy in your thought and you are concern with fighting back and forget God's peace is in you and your real intention.

You are directed by the ego concept of *self-importance* and feeling special. You are as equal as anyone. Next time, when you feel being put down, or being insulted by an unfriendly gesture take a deep breath and chanting God sound "*ah*" that will cool you down and return to your original intention that God is in you and feel the peace. You respect yourself is an innate state, to love and understand the world around you. You must eliminate any idea of loving to win and always winning. However, in the physical world there is no win, win situation and at the end nobody wins it all. In a competition, seemingly you may win it today, but tomorrow is a new day. The present becomes the past.

A new challenger and new circumstance will always arise like the rising sun in the horizon. Winning or losing is only temporary, and when you meditate on the inner peace from within and you have a *winner's heart*. The winner's heart dwells with God.

When you are less concern about winning or losing anymore, then all of sudden there are more victories that will emerge in your life to surprise you. Remember; do not look for specialty because this will cause upheaval and non-peace in your heart. You are always seeking for a challenger and you could not perceive what is presented to you in the present moment. When you can't find another competition, then you self proclaim to be the only winner in the world. The reality is it might not always be the case, the world is rotating and the *wheel of life* is never stops moving and new technology, new knowledge, and new champion will always emerge, but you never know. You must feel God's peace and let go of your need and control and let nature take its course and more will emerge to you when you expect less. Allow the invisible driving force guiding and directing your life with purpose of serving God and others. Do not let guilty memories manipulate you. God has given you great variety of spiritual gifts. Manage them wisely so that God's generosity can flow you and transcends it and benefits to others.

Let God gives you a fresh start and cling on *Him* to clear your record. Let go of worry, fear, and lack and do not hold onto the pain of resentment and bitterness. You must learn from it and let it go.

You don't need to have more to be satisfied, and then you can consider sharing with another. A willingness to share your fortune with another person will demolish selfishness in your conscious mind.

The willingness to give and share with others will create and attract more of good karma into your life, because, what goes around comes around. The cause and effect of the *Law of Karma* will record what you do on the data sheet and consequently, an unlimited abundance will come back.

When you think of achievements, it is unlikely you do not think of all the awards that you could accumulate. In fact, your successes and accomplishments do not originate from you, but from **The Source**. It is God, who gives you this inborn talent to accomplish the success in your life. You simply use your innate talent obtained from **The Source** to materialize it in the physical world.

The less credential you accumulate the more you are aligned to your *Source* and all ventures you have created and accomplished are guided by the invisible *Source*, and then you feel free to achieve more with a grateful mind and the connection to the invisible power of God.

Your reputation is not accumulated by you, but it resonates in the conscious minds of the world. You understand that you have no control over the opinion of others. The truth is you will have conversation with many people and you hear many different opinions about you. Some agree with you, but some don't. You need to stay focused on your intention; listen to what your heart tells you. If you are overly concerned on how others see you, you will be influenced by other opinions instead of staying with your original intended thought.

You will derail yourself and go back to your old thinking patterns, which is controlled by the ego. You try to prove to others on how powerful and masterful you are and pushing your energy on maintaining your top reputation among your rivals. Again, you will realize that it only pushes you behind, because you are not concentrating on your origin intention in each moment, but are driven by fear of an unrealistic expectation and concentrating on achieving the recognition and success. Regardless of the course, you are misaligned with your inner consciousness and feeling struggle to climb the ladder to triumph.

You need to redirect your thoughts and concentrate effectively to attract the dreams and desires into your life. You must change your inner dialogue and refine your thought and return to what God intends for you.

You may extend more of what you learn and implement a new dialogue, when you are communicating with your *Source*. You observe your thought waves when you tap into this inner dialogue with your *Inner Knowing*. For example, you thought of being alone and helpless, instead of transcending this unhealthy and unhappy negative message to the *Universe*. Immediately, you have transmuted your thought patterns to attract more peace and happiness into your life.

When you quit struggling, you will meet someone to teach you something special to improve your life. Chance of meeting the right people to aid you is wide open. This will happen at the right time and at the right place. You may already know that the vibrational alignment with your *Inner Source* is a positive energy. You have activated the power of the *Law of Magnetic Energy* and the *Power of Success* to assist your desired outcome. When you chose to stay in the higher energy field you chose the best possible solution to obtain the results needed.

It is important for you to continue to align with your subconscious mind to create more positive energies and you know that your disruption and emotional feelings are in misalignment with your *Source* and will increase the chance of upset and despair. You are not channeling in the right direction, because you are constantly focused on the negative thought and your energy system are being disrupted.

However, you have choices on how to unleash any condition and manifest what you desire, removing blocks to embrace with your positive vibrations, and melt the iceberg and making room for peace and fulfillment you have always wanted.

When you feel depressed and despaired or even lonely, this is not part of your true nature and you need to monitor your lower energy. You can always reject thoughts that are not compatible with your *Source*.

You can always move towards **The Source** and speak to God about your difficulties, confusions, and despairs. You will hear your answer in silence. Your *Source* will listen, sustain and reassure all your needs are always met. You replace God in your mind and let God transforms you inwardly by a completed change of your mind. Then, you will know the will of God.

You must pay attention to your vibrational thoughts that cause the lower energy to weaken your position. You need to watch your lower energy levels, never allow them to weaken your power to think correctly, and ultimately pull you away from your subconscious force. If you do notice you're feeling blue, discomfort, anxiety, disquiet and uneasy then, you must immediately re-align to your *Source*, regain your momentum and higher energy vibration as you continue to adjust your thoughts to eliminate contrasting desires that disrupt the experiences waiting for you in your life journey.

Your real security is your alignment with **The Source.** God will constantly watches over your response to people, success, conflict, failure, illness and *He* will make sure everything is fine for you. He wants you making conscious connection with *Him* and feels His omnipresence and love. He wants to know you have *Him* in your heart. Every day is an important day and every next day is a growth opportunity to develop your love and thinks of God and depends on *Him.*

Finally, Self-respect can be achieved when we learn to respect and love ourselves. This is because no one can understand us better than ourselves. Next time, if you are down a little, and looking for energy to uplift your confidence, you don't need to look further, but meditate from within and get the answer. Then, you learn your own growth and honor your own perfection.

When you have God in your heart those undesired thoughts will be overrule, but if it occurs you simply say it aloud, *"I control my own thoughts, and I don't need your help now!"*

You should always view difficulties and obstacles as a challenge and do not be afraid to accept fail. You can always transform difficulties into triumph and trust that the *Light of God* is always shinning on you.

Chapter Four
~The Mind on Money~

Money is the realm of spirituality. However, consider money is a form of energy, it can possibly be a seed, and used wisely, and positively, it can expose enormous *Light*.

It may be a good thought to give a percentage of your income to charity so that it will bring nourishment to your life. It is based on the idea of material reality, called **malchut**, which is defined as an expression of desire for oneself alone. Therefore, give a percentage of your net income will eliminate the desire for oneself alone, and help to connect to the high levels of spiritual energy in your money.

Money is the product for exchange of goods and services in the material world. Money has its value only when merchants and bankers add the values in front of the "*zero*," and then the paper money has its authentic value. If money is not accepted by the merchants, then it has lost its true value and become valueless.

How do you keep an eye on your earning money? It's practical to create a personal preference of saving money for emergency. It is thoughtless to spend all your funds without saving them. In the beginning, you may find it difficult to save money, because you might not have a vivid pay check.

Yet, you still can do it with the power of intention. Instruct and guide your conscious mind to obey your order. Convey your conscious mind becomes your obedient servant and peaceful ally.

Then, you transform vibrational thoughts into action and begin saving money. Eventually, it becomes a routine and an easy thing to do.

Consequently, you have impressed your subconscious mind to collaborate with you. You begin to perceive the joy from within. You attract more abundance into your life, as your income rises and consider increasing the amount of money you can save. This positive action will activate the *Law of Magnetic Energy* and the power of success to bring more richness and prosperity to you without making an effort. Most significantly, your decision to save money will give rise to opportunity to improve your life style and eliminate your feeling of scarcity, uplifting your self-esteem and confidence. Ultimately, it enlightens more joys and successes into your life.

It is beyond a reasonable doubt that there is no scarcity, but abundance for everyone. Scarcity is only an illusion in your conscious mind and is the egos way of thinking to confuse you.

It is egos judgment of pessimist that rules your beliefs system. Your unwillingness to do anything to improve life has vanished and your deliberated state *"as is"* situation.

In your ego system, you believe that you were a natural born loser. Because of your unmoved situation, all you hope for is to receive a few pennies from people walk by you on the street and making no effort to transform or uplift your life. Eventually, this wasteful life becomes habits; your job is to earn a few pennies on the street. The subconscious mind registers this idea and setup the limitation on what you can earn. Consequently, your opportunity to open this portal is closed eternally and your destiny is now set. (For example, this person sitting on the street corner, ask people for pennies and tell people walk by him have a good day. But, does he have a good day himself? I can imagine the kind of a day, he has. He focuses his energies on this single goal: bag cents. His activities are not helping him evaluate his current situation. He concentrates his efforts and energy by sitting there and asked for penny. Does he ever wonder if his current situation will lead him to live a useful life? His life is ineffective without purpose and never goes anywhere. He has trashed his life.)

However, when a person refuse to accept poverty that his life is not on a pre-set destiny, and he has consciously changed his thought and it will transform his fate. In fact, you can modify your fate by using your vibrational thoughts and determine to change, you realize life offers you many choices; you are free to create the life you desire. You are affirming your success by taking steadfast action and aligning with your *Source* and assign more time meditate on develop a mutual relationship with God.

Now when you consider that there is nothing more important than your emotional state to make you feel inner bliss and liberates you, you have presently decided to deliberately create and broaden your opportunities to meet helpful people, better circumstances, and ultimately, you will emerge in the right place at the right time. Most importantly, your self-esteem and self-confidence have improved tremendously. As confidence increases, you begin to learn to honor and celebrate yourself with self-respect and know that you are perfect. Your willingness to motivate yourself to do more have opened windows of opportunities into your life and this allows you to live comfortably.

Because life improves, as your conscious awareness is focused on attracting more successes and prosperities and strengthening your intention on living truly and abundantly. You manage to amend your poverty consciousness to wealth consciousness. You accepted the old self was your past and did not fit your profile now.

Your beliefs and willingness to trust is a key in receiving desire results. You make changes and accept who you are and being in the now. Acceptance of who you are and the power to eliminate all bad habits and self-defeating concepts and unwanted attachments that could possibly block your life. Ultimately, you have impressed upon the subconscious to re-write your blueprint and willing to assist you to the end. Hence, you are aware of ideas that are deliberately set in the mind and will influence your beliefs system.

However, you must be determined to change your beliefs system and aligning with the ideas and details that you desire to live abundantly. Because of your action, the *Law of Magnetic Energy* and the power of evolution begins to draw more good things into your life. You continue to focus your mind on subconscious thoughts; the more likeliness comes to you. For you to live in conscious awareness is ultimately to live peacefully. Rapidly, a wider window and portal is opened without any effort. All because you trust your creative power to create the kind of life, you want. You are being host to God and receive conscious peace.

In the consciousness, you are aware of **The Source** dwelling within and nobody can give you this natural born power. The *Law of Magnetic Energy* and the *Law of Success* will bring anything you create. It is through the vibration of your conscious thoughts that are in tune with you and your *Source*, to bring the harmonious result to meet your heart's desire.

Money is an internal realm and therefore money is spirit. The extra money you earn, you could give to others will render more money and abundance to befall upon you. When you give money to help others with joy, the *Universe* will know because it is from your heart. You give something to others when you feel God's peace. It is supported by the *Universal Law of Giving and Receiving*.

However, you can always find a way to give something to the needy, but it is not limited to just money only *"the sky"* is the limit. The art of giving is when you have done something to help others and you feel joyful and blissful inside.

The power of manifesting more money is *"giving."* Using money to help people without expecting anything in return that is the greatest joy that you give to **The Source** inside. When you give money to help people with joy and you have the whole Universes support. Because, you have created a positive energy flow to you and becomes your blessings. Your generosity lends to receiving more abundance and demonstrates the faith and trust you have in yourself and others.

Belief is seeing, seeing is believed. You begin to help others because you perceive yourself doing so in the mind's eye and you feel an urge to do it. It is the most powerful thing that you give to yourself and your *Source*. Because of your good deeds it will influence others consciousness to do likewise.

The Universal Mind acknowledges the higher infinite energy and because of this collective energy ultimately will return to the outer world and will become everyone's blessings, which are bestowed from Heaven. Because God is peace and peace dwells in everyone's heart. Finally, if you desire to live abundantly, you must perceive the abundance in you. You must be aware of what you have contemplated in your subconscious mind.

Because, what you contemplate in your subconscious mind is the life style you want to go to. But, you must be aware that you combine your thought energy and your own vibrational powers to indicate you are not going around the block, but taking control of your mind to reach the right destination. When you are aligned with the energy of your subconscious mind, you have opened to yourself, and super charged your energy to receive love, health, wealth, wisdom, and success. You have also opened to experience enthusiasm, passion, clarity, and vitality. It is your nature to feel inner peace. You begin reaching for relief, moment-by-moment and thought by thought until your subconscious mind absorbs every single message and creating a permanent and exciting transformation into your life.

You feel vigorously motivated with a new empowered belief in yourself. You ignite the passion in love life and your relationships. You instantly eliminate self doubt and completely let go of negative thinking and begin taming the ego and shift to the awareness of **The Source**.

The nature, the air you breathe, the trees and the flowers are signs that life is to enjoy and this nature is full of Divine light and abundance, now simply observe what God has created for you and its limitless resources. You are living abundantly, there is nothing to worry, and scarcity is just an illusion, and believes everything is in the utmost capable hands of the omnipotence and omnipresence of God.

It feels like you always want it to be, eventually it will be as you seen it. You have started to attract more of what you want, like the rain dropping into the river so joyful and peaceful.

Furthermore, watch and see that your life has changed, as your energy shifts. By placing your attention on what you want to manifest rather than staying in the lower energy field that you experience, then you make a decision to connect to your intention and divert your thought to the positive energy field, which brings attributes of your *Source* to the presence of higher energy. You remove any doubt in you and fill yourself in the situation and the intention you want to fulfill, and feel the presence of peace and love. You are what you choose to be in any circumstance and your choice to be truly peaceful, and feel the joy and blissful.

You bring the intention of peace in you and refusing to judge them. You will then start to look forward to being in that situation and feel enlightened. You'll enjoy the work you do and if anything emerges to annoy you, then you simply fill it with peace and love instead. You feel like quietly responding with harmony and limit your own opinion to the minimum, and simply let the matter drop.

By changing the way you see and think the objects you look at transform. When your observation is based on the limitation, scarcity and then the current situation is the determining factor, which determines your life ultimate outcome. Extending to a larger view will show the effect of the physical world? Your ability to succeed and live abundantly, you must release your hidden potential and begin to tap into the enormous power waiting for you and believe that you can accomplish what you set your sights on. You can do anything if you set your mind to by using the power of imagination.

All limits are eliminated through the power of your belief and possibly based on negative structures. It can be changed, if you believe you can and have faith in these invisible powers. It is time to liberate that limiting belief that you have deliberately chosen and become aware of new life unfolding to you and begin now.

We share the Universal abundance through the connection with the Divine's power, and the energy you decide to focus on determines whether you have seen abundance or scarcity surrounding you.

In addition, your unwillingness to see things change, may be hinder by your past beliefs. When you realize your inner purpose of your infinite power is to live successfully and abundantly, you will gain more inner prosperity and riches and love your soul.

In conclusion, there are no limits to the image you can manifest and visualize. You can easily rotate your life in an instant. The freedom and determination to choose when that happens is yours. Guide yourself to take action now that will create a better future. Live in the present and take that step to move forward, and live in that moment. The present is the "*Now*" and you will never need to wait for anything to happen to you.

Chapter Five
~The Power of Thought~

Your vibrational thoughts are powerful; it will bring you anything your heart's desire. However, if your desire is to win lotto, then you must buy a lottery ticket. Fortune comes to you when you transcend your thoughts into actions. Then, your action will transcend it into your own physical reality and manifest many countless opportunities into your life.

You have the abilities to use the imagination, to perceive images in your mind and transcend them into your actual reality. By visualizing an event, a situation, we see cars, houses, money, and anything you can image will attract to you. We perceive it in our imagination what we want and it will happen overtime. It is a day dream, but actually it is the process of the *power of thought*.

Now with your eyes closed take a three deep breath, lucid your mental mind, let go of all clutters and slowly draw your attention to a creative image you wish to create. In your mind's eye you attempt to create a visualize image of a lotto ticket you bought has contains the six winning numbers. You continue to hold that image in a solid form and perceive that it is flowing in front of you.

Once you created a vivid image of the ticket, think of the six numbers you have in front of you and see that it will match with the drawing numbers at the present. Your visualization should be strong and a firm belief that you have a winning ticket. You must believe this is not merely thought, but it can transform into your own physical reality. You must continue to hold a positive mental attitude and let your thoughts entertain this idea long enough to materialize. You are part of Universal creation and whatever thoughts you create and holding it at certain time frame will change the balance of energy and environment around you. Therefore, the power of thoughts affects the influence of the nature and the *Law of Magnetic Energy* to materialize it. After countless draws, the same number you bought was drawn and incredible success just flows your way and you are the winner. Now you know you can trigger this anytime the continual flow of money into your life.

However, a certain element must be met, before you can accumulate materialize objects into your life. For example, if you desire to plant your crops into the ground water them every day and let the crop receive the ingredients needed to grow stronger, and healthier. You can also send positive energy to the crops to grow better. Most importantly, monitor and remove all clutters growing around the crops. When the harvest time finally arrives, you will have an abundant supply.

Before you can begin to grow anything on the farm land, preparation is needed and the right seeds of thoughts are needed to have a successful crop.

You have perceived how many crops you desire to cultivate in your mind's eye. A clear picture emerges in your vibrational thoughts that you perceive and abundant outcome. Your emotions indicate you are vibrating a higher energy; it matches and reflects in your inner state and reflects back to the physical world.

Because of your positive emotions it translates the power of thoughts into action and influence the environment around you and the balance of energy connected with nature and the *Law of Magnetic Energy*, join with the *Law of Allowing* will result in whatever you have cultivated on your farm land. Finally, since your emotions are in alignment with the *Universal Source* and a passionate eye on your plan and the power to create the idea situation can be expected.

You know you are unique and your uniqueness is different from others. In fact, no single experiences are similar because of our uniqueness and talents born within us. One becomes the President of the United States and the other, just a normal wealthy happy Joe. It is all preset for you to tap into what kind of life you desire to live, while you experience your soul purpose on Earth. I am not suggesting you compare one with another because each individual is unique and our uniqueness is used to fulfill God's assignment and fulfill everything in our heart's desire.

The power of thought is connected with your *Inner Source* to receive these calm and peaceful feelings in the mind. Having a special place in your home, where you can relax and meditate on God is the most wonderful moment you can imagine. It is your sacred place, where you share your emotions alone with your *Source* during the time of reflection. If you are like me, I have a sacred place in my home, which I use to develop my relationship with the Divine. Three years ago, I set aside a room for devotion, I began to feel tranquil, and the stillness, as a result, more joys, and blissfulness occurred to me. I understand struggle is unnecessary for survival. Everything that happens has a Divine's purpose. Every morning I spend some time talking to my *Source*, showing my appreciation and gratitude. I do it before I start my writing. It becomes a habit, because I feel connected with my *Source*. As I sit at the LCD monitor screen, I ask my *Source* to guide me and writing begins to flow through to me word for word and sentence by sentence until the end of the day. I know this writing is going to be a good medium for many readers. My purpose is to inform them of the knowledge that I have gained with **The Source** and let them explore the content of my experiences and to share this book globally. That is my creative purpose in doing this great work for **The Source** and others.

Are you aware that we have sixty thousand thoughts per day and two per second and many of these thoughts are swept into your mind without notice?

Some of these thoughts are beneficial, but some are excessive, pessimistic thoughts and revisit the mind. Often, we battle the mind to bring us harmonious thoughts instead of hurtful feelings.

The conscious mind is the physical mind that directs your thought into action in the external world while the subconscious mind manifested, assisted, and confirms your thoughts into actual reality. The subconscious mind will only act upon what is sent from the mental state. However, the subconscious mind is the innate source that can bring our desires and actions into reality. So, why is it so important to apply your thinking patterns with the subconscious? Because, the subconscious is the *Inner Source* that connects you with the *Mind of God*. When you and **The Source** are constantly connected, then immediately feel the bliss and peace in you. There is no need to battle, because you have reached the center of yourself, so that peace can work with you to create what is needed. Since there is no lack of scarcity and ennui will not set in to hurt you and nothing is missing? If there is nothing on the horizon, therefore there is no worry or fear, but peace in the mind.

Your peace of mind will help you to calm your every day stresses. It is through your *Inner Knowing* that constantly connected to the Divine, which brings the vibrational harmony, joy, and peace in you. You can ask for its service at anytime you feel like, but you must invite it in to assist you. **The Source** will not interfere with your life, only by invitation.

But, where is this Source?

This incredible *Inner Source* dwells in your heart. It quietly assists you behind the screen to meet your needs and daily activities. It removes you from danger when your life is in jeopardy. You simply have to listen to that quiet voice guiding you and follow it. You will not be disappointed.

Often times, when you apply thoughts with the conscious mind, the results turn out to be disappointing, from what you desire.

Why?

This is because you battle with your mind to get what you want, which is totally opposite to peace condition, and what could benefit you. Your subconscious mind is in misalignment with **The Source** and is being disturbed. You do not feel the peace and tranquility within and constantly battled with the material things that you wish to obtain, which is beyond your control and estimated time. When the things you desire did not occur, then you become very upset and disappointed.

You are constantly fighting with the ego mind and neglect the important part of love and peace in you. Therefore, your emotions are affected and you are not in a state of consciousness to think of a solution to resolve your undesirable events.

The more you worry about the problem, the more you keep the solution in you. Think of a scenario in the recent past, which disturbed your mind and left you confused and misdirected. Immediately, you will feel distress and discontent. A negative thought memory has ignited and jammed your subconscious mind, which is opposite to what you are seeking but rather giving you a sense of insecurity and discontentment. Now turn your thought to a particular event that you were delighted and enjoyed. Imagine a virtual picture of you just signing a major contract with Dell and receiving a check of $xxx, xxx. Visualize the success and wealth that you have and feel the joy and peacefulness that you attracted and the *Universe* has granted your wish. It illustrates that whatever you decided about this world is the way your world will be. The joy and happiness reflected on your face from the inner state of mind to the outer consciousness. You say to yourself quietly, "*oh, I am happy.*" The above are the two illustrated thoughts you might have in your mind, which constantly affect the way you choose to live your life. They are very influential and effective. You have to decide, which one is right for you. The choice is yours. Because, life is about a series of choices, before a decision is made it is an illusion, but after you have determined your choice, then all these illusions will vanish. The Universe continues to reinforce your final decision about life and provide all things and events that go along with that decision. Life is abundant. The *Universe* will return to you all your needs because of your decisions. It is only when we open to influx and accepts new ideas and concepts, that the *Universe* offers a variety of ways to provide our needs and desires.

Remember that you are part of the Universal creation, so whatever you think of can and will be created with your intention in a harmonious way, because the *Universal Mind* will only work with harmonious and a peaceful state of mind.

The *Universal Mind* is in the state of endless supply. It constantly works for you at your service without ceasing. We are treated equally in that *Fertile Energy Field* through the invisible power of the *Universal Source*. However, you must stay in the higher energy field to manifest your desire and intention.

Everything in the *Universe* is created by energy and energy is the source of power to all connections. Sooner, the conditions are met and become mature it will bring those conditions into the material world, and will become everyone's reality. The *Universal Mind* will include anyone, but if you are not receiving what you desire, it is because you could not see yourself living abundantly with infinite opportunities and the possibilities opening to you. Changes your mind to positive thoughts and the *Universe* will guide each moment as it shall unfolds and bring more positive events into your life.

If you create a visual image, of what you desire in your mind and transcend it into the *Universe* to obtain what you wish. Then, you must stay attentive and observe any resistant forces preventing you from getting the abundance in your life.

After you have released your desire to the *Universe*, you must guide your thoughts to stay in that intended energy field and do not let any unsteady negative thoughts penetrate into your mind to influence you. It is best being contented with your thoughts, and knowing exactly how to achieve this degree of maintaining a successful manifestation. When you feeling good, then you know that, you are allowing, attracting, and receiving everything. You must be aware of your own creative energy and reality, and aligned with the *Divine Light Power* to uphold your heart's desire.

Since reality follows thought, therefore any success and abundance is possible when you are not too concerned on how these acquisitions will come. However, thoughts in your mind can become barriers if you have an illusion of scarcity. The resistant force created a negative energy preventing what is to come into your life. It is your mental disharmony and misalignment with your own translation of insufficiency. Your thoughts are misaligned from **The Source** and receiving what you want becomes unlikely until you are reconnected again. The solution is to erase stored memory from your subconscious and then everything becomes possible.

Reprogram your conscious thought with positive impulses to express a new life through your subconscious mind. What is sent to the subconscious mind is giving freely.

Your feelings actually affect the power of your experience and sustain your goal to take action. The connection is looking beyond your energy and get closer to the nature of your inner peace. It is a place where miracles can take place and live with balance.

Assume, right now you want to create love and relationships into your life. Your positive feelings indicate that you are in alignment with your subconscious mind, and your thoughts filled with inner peace and joy, then the *Law of Magnetic Energy* goes to work and draws love into your life.

You are the creative power of your own thoughts and desires. In every moment, that you live is a creative moment with different experience. The positive attitude has inspired you to create conditions that make all your desires possible. The *Universal Mind* knows your needs when positive thought are manifested into the *Universe* it matches all your needs, desires and conditions and you simply be still and wait and believe the object is yours or will be yours.

The expansion of this *Universe* depends on the creation of new ideas and then the *Universal Law of Magnetic Energy* will bring the new ideas and desires into light through the *power of allowing* and accepting this freely.

Many people have asked why their desires do not manifest to them. It is because they do not have faith that their ideas can come true. What you ask is actually given to you in a spiritual sense. It is because everything is created in the spirit realm first before it enters into the physical world.

However, when it returns, you are neither aware of it nor ready to receive it. This is because perhaps the moment it returns, you have already changed your mind or implemented a new idea in your thoughts. Therefore, you feel you are not receiving it. Again, it is a moment to moment feeling and you must make a conscious connection to your original thoughts and mentally see them and the conditions you wish it to be, and the *Law of Magnetic Energy* will obey your order and materialize it to you.

When you create a vibrational thought you must be very specific and knowing precisely what you desire. Then, you visualize a clear picture in your mind's eye and believe you will receive this in the physical form. You must continue to contemplate on that same desire and aligned with your intentions and believe everything is in alignment with your idea. Most importantly, it shows no indication that you can't fulfill it. Because, your energy is focused and you have always stayed in your manifestation thought field and everything can transform into crystal reality.

All things are invisible to physical eyes until it is materialize and solidified. Therefore, when you begin to visualize internally, you have activated the power of your thought within.

When a thought is activated, it matches with other collective consciousness in the manifestation field; your creative power will assist you in activating the creative principle of the *Law of Magnetic Energy* and blend this with the *Law of Harmony* and the *Law of Manifestation* until your desires are materialize into light.

You are always return to activate your original thoughts, eventually, it becomes the great attracting power, and then your mental image is certain to be projected upon the screen in your physical world and an exact reproduction of a picture in your mind. However, the *Law of Magnetic Energy* will continue to guide you focusing on the intended energy thought and subsequently, activating the picture in your mind. Because, you have stayed focus on the *Higher Energy Field* and the *Law of Magnetic Energy* will fill the vibration of this reality.

When you thought of buying things you desire, immediately you think of lack. Therefore, you always hesitate to transform your thoughts into action. In other words, your thought and desire do not have a reality equivalent. You have to break free from those limitations and allow your thought process to carry forward. Then, a world of new opportunities will emerge to you. This thought will have a strong support from the *Law of Magnetic Energy* and attract more things to you. This is because it matches with your intention and the desire you wish to create. You have activated something you don't realize, but it is activated now.

You approach the *Law of Magnetic Energy* through the subconscious mind, rather than through the mental state and you discover **The Source** energy within. You have allowed your new destination to take its place to become influential and everything starts to happen effectively for you, because of your trust and faith in the ideas and the power of your creative thoughts.

As your confidents builds this momentum becomes an original power of energy. You will receive everything you desire at your finger tips. You experience more love, joy, and happiness in every aspect of your life.

Your thoughts will change as you change your belief system. Your whole life will also be affected because of an internal shift in your thought and reflect your external environmental changes. Your feelings are very important to boost up the materialization of your desire. Because, if you are always feeling negative about yourself, your self-esteem will drop and become too difficult for you to believe anything can be created and manifested. However, if you rise beyond that low self-confidence then immediately, you have transformed your energy to a higher energy field and are aware of opportunities presenting themselves to you and match with your intention to create incredible events in your life. When you are in the *Higher Energy Field* you can focus on the energy of your choice and your personal preference. You will continue to focus on positive feelings and the *Law of Magnetic Energy* will continue to bring more similar thoughts and you are free to accept or reject this energy.

Your fulfillment can be reached only when you have fully accepted and decided this is what you desire without any reservation.

Your feelings let you know how much energy you can draw to your desire in this moment. They let you know your thought has failed or succeeded to match with the subject you focus on is near or distance from you. A feeling of passion or enthusiasm is focused on the presence of stillness and trusting the message you hear and have a strong urge to act on this. When you are passionately focused on doing something good and the subject of your desire will gain all the energy needed to attract more of these influential energy to bring your desire without resistance.

On the contrary, when you focus on disgust or backlash then your environmental thought will be granted. You then attract more negative energy during these states of mind, whether you are allowing or disallowing this. You are responding to negative thoughts and the effect of this becomes your own reality. Your conscious thoughts constantly manifesting the negative energy into substance from formless and are directed towards you. You have unknowingly activated the *Law of Magnetic Energy* to bring more undesired events to that environment with the same power. You realize whatever you manifest will be sustained until your weakest link has been replaced with a better energy thought. Remember, you are living in a world of thoughts.

You must be aware of the rate of your thoughts in order to change the integration of ideas and concepts streaming into your mind. As your thoughts deepen and reach higher levels of intuitive thinking. The brain cells are refined and creating a better conduit to allow unity of energy thoughts. You feel the vibrational harmony in you, because of your unity with self and your thoughts.

Your emotional feelings will show that there is a strong connection with the negative thought through the sensation of your body's gesture and tells you that you are off the manifestation. Your negative states produced the power of unwanted energy. Since the *Law of Magnetic Energy* will not decide for you, but only match and sustain what you ask for. If you desire continue to stay in the *lower magnetic field*, it becomes impossible for you to change your course, because the higher and the lower frequency don't blend together. Therefore, it is unlikely they will meet each other on the same thought field.

Since thoughts are very effective, therefore negative thoughts should be limited to minimize the confusion in the mind so that only the essence of positive energy is influence and will be refined and transcend to the *Universe*.

Negative thoughts that have no intrinsic value and can cause physical, emotional and mental illness in you and should be avoided. Eliminate any negative energy and substitute them with love.

Love is from the God and we should focus on this to create a pleasant environment and to build upon our abilities to communicate.

One way that can help you to focus on positive energy is to handover everything to your *Source* and *God* will look after everything for you. In most circumstance, when we feel inharmonious and act on it and this brings more confusion and uneasiness, which bring obstacles and limitations. You must decide to let go, and let nature take its course. A solution emerges to resolve your problem, because you are allowing love to replace your fears and worries. You must be aware of the roots of your negative thoughts to eliminate any untrue desire. You are consciously tied to the dream that is connected and resonates in you. There is nothing in the world that can stop you from attaining things you desire except for your decision to manifest the opposite. Indifference can derail the misalignment with your *Inner Knowing*. But, you always know how to find the weakest part and cut the connection with these roots and filled it with love. When you fill your adverse situations with love and listen to the *Inner Guidance* and this inspired voice will guide you out of turmoil and adversity. You must be aware of your situation, because in the end all you have is to face yourself. However, when you are truly submitting your difficulties to God and you will know you have the abilities to change your own thought and behavior.

Since you have the abilities to control how you responded to events in your life. You are also controlling the balance of both positive and negative influences and find a beneficial accrue with both sides of the dial. However, if the event happens in your life is beyond your comprehension, then it is wise to let go of resistance. The infinite power of the *Universe* will help and sustain you to resolve your problems. Because our physical abilities are limited and we cannot win all the time. There are circumstances we cannot resolve ourselves without "*special help.*" This incredible help comes from the invisible force of the *Universe*, which will fulfill all your needs and concerns. It is the power you can trust and rely upon. **The Source** will not ask you for anything back. All you need to do is trust and have faith in its power.

Despite your efforts to live abundantly, you should surrender to **The Source** and work in concert with *Him* in waking you from your infallible state and finding your direction again. Surrendering does not mean that you need to sacrifice everything, but you simply let *The Source* guide you to do what is right for you. There are portals you can use, however, surrender to the one you need most that can help you to face anything in life other than rely upon the uncertainty in you.

Surrender to God means giving your trust and faith to him. You can fall back fully, and have faith and trust that God will catch you. Faith is complete trust in him. Trust eliminates doubt, allowing a miracle to take place. Prayer is the medium of miracles. We simply have to trust and believe.

What inspires you most will lead to the determination of the power of your success. The motivation and determination that you give your power to succeed is consciously connected with your desire to implement something you always wish for, or where you want to be. However, in this case it is the thought vibration that manifests this power within you.

Your thought vibrations, which are consciously aligned with **The Source,** as you continue to allow this positive energy to develop and let your intention grow and become more mature, your progress towards the achievement is empowered by your power of success to enjoy life.

When you have a strong desire to succeed and believe you deserve it, then the *Universe* will support and make it happen and nobody can take away this determination from you. You cannot cease to create a list of preferences. It is your life experiences that help you to determine both internal and external levels in your personal viewpoints, which are submitted consciously or subconsciously and is heard and answered by **The Source**.

After you have submitted your request to the *Universe* pay special attention to your feelings of joy that arise to indicate your progress and the command of your own thoughts, which are aligned with your *Inner Source*.

Thought is a living force. Thought is energy emanating from the *Inner Source*. It is very powerful and has the potential to bring everything into your life. Thoughts can change from moment to moment without you noticing it. Thoughts can bring you prosperity and constructive powers to you. On the contrary, your thoughts can also be destructive force when used unwisely. Your body is the reflection of your thoughts. Every thought you think about will affect the healthy condition in your body.

Diseases and illnesses is the reflection of your mind. It means your thoughts are focused on negative vibrations such as worry, fear, and scarcity. These negative thoughts affect every organ in your body. You feel fatigue, moodiness, and pessimistic. This negative thought can make you become unenthusiastic in your views and what you see in the physical world. Your mind is full of negative vibrations and change is unlikely. You must understand your thought is what you become. If you meditate your thought on compassion, kindness, truthfulness, and integrity, eventually you will have these qualities of character in you. It is reflected in your external conscious state of mind from your inner consciousness. Soon more calmness and peacefulness emerges in your mind and you blend this peaceful character into your destiny.

Men think all the time and as men thinks an action is brought forward affecting his future events. Every action has its cause and effect. The cause of one-man decision can affect many men's lives. That is the power of his thoughts.

Will our thoughts and actions affect our future events?

I will let the Universe unfold new ideas and opportunities and will see each moment to learn and grow.

The endless power of men's thoughts can be activated by three activities—desire, action, and destiny. Desires stimulate thoughts, thoughts transform into an action, and action becomes one's destiny. We fill our subconscious minds with product conditioning and there is unlimited supply. We carry over into each morning all of our desires and dreams into reality as the day unfold. Every day we make progress, because you are focused clearly on your destination and have learned to eliminate worry and doubt from the mind and with each consistence step will bring more positive events into your life.

There are various ways you can guide your mind from your disrupting thoughts. This is accomplished with the mind through concentration, and visualization and execution of your intent. Look at the source of pain on your face and say, you no longer control the way you perceive life. I will not decide what is defined as positive or negative, but I will let the *Universe* unfold new ideas and opportunities and will see each moment as an opportunity to learn and evolve. Change your old thoughts and habits and replace them with new expressions and concepts emerging from your *Inner Self*. Your positive thinking has inspired the subconscious mind to infuse you with unlimited ideas and confidence. Each expression is expressed with a positive attitude in life, which attracts more blessings from the *Universe*. Experiencing and witnessing your own nature, because you are imbued with the creative power of the *Universal Creative Life Force*.

The *Law of Magnetic Energy* is a very powerful Universal law and is associated with the power of thought. The theory of like-minds attracts liked-mindedness and shares the common views to be seem by others.

Our minds have the drawing power to attract the likeness towards us through the power of visible and the invisible Universal forces. These two forces can assist us to achieve success and abundance in the best of ways. Spirit guides us with this invisible force. Our lives work out to be just right. But, in fact these are **The Source** energies in action.

Affirm now you are ready to commit all the abundance that the *Universe* will allow and you have infused and empowered this abundance into your body, mind, and spirit.

The Universal laws of the *Law of Magnetic Energy* attracts and matches your thoughts to your personal choice, and guides and connects them to you without judging your decision.

Everything in the *Universe* is made of energy and energy can travel through the atmosphere without limitation. Therefore, it is possible that thought vibrations could travel from mind to mind without time-space limitation. The best ways to explain this is that it vibrates through the power of the subconscious mind and can send vital messages to other consciousness.

First, it flows through a subtle mind, transcends into the atmosphere, and fills the outer space with a strong energy, and then the message is transmitted into the subconscious mind of that person. The person senses this message through his sixth sense. This practice is influenced while entering your inner silence to direct the transmission and to activate the vibration of those thought to be sent to other minds is known as telepathy.

A person must know and expect the transmission of message sent to him and should not unknowingly send messages without the awareness of the effect it will have on other minds.

We think all the time to transform our desires into action. Meditation is one of the methods you can use to control and direct your thoughts towards your purpose. Everything happens for a particular reason, but we are not conscious of it until the event has happened and it becomes obvious. Simply put, everything was staged before we knew it. You must be aware that as you sow so shall you reap. What you plant in your spiritual thoughts is what you will get with the impulse results. We are the only mammal that uses words to communicate with each other. Therefore, the use of words has an impact on every one of us. The proper transitional word will help you in a situation or eliminate a bad habit. These transition words can assist you in your thought processes to know exactly the word you should employ in action, in difficult situations and in your speech and some words have the power to transform your mind to peace from disturbance.

One man thoughts and action can transform everything into turmoil because of the power of his thoughts. His thought and belief is full of greed, jealousy, and abhorrence. In the past and the present we still go through many wars. It is because one-man's ambition was transformed and affected by the behavior of another person indirectly or intangibly.

Many tyrants are able to charm, manipulate and misused their powers throughout ancient history to make false gains and are still happening in some countries. It is because one did not use their thoughts correctly and properly, but rather to use their thoughts in a greedy and destructive manner.

Men always learn valuable lessons through violence and grief before triumph. When we learn to use peaceful thoughts towards each other, a real peace will emerge. It fulfills the purpose of why we are here to carry God's peace. Perhaps in the moment it is easy to say than to do. I believe until the entire human race is willing to submit their indifferences, and pride and join together to endorse love and peace in their hearts, and feel God's presence from within.

In fact, peace is obtained through the thought in our minds. Harmony is reflected and expressed in our hearts to the outer world. It means we have the abilities to control our thoughts and to determine how our actions can affect us. We don't need to wait for the unexpected events to happen to feel others pain and using proper actions to prevent any accident to occur.

Life is an unfoldment and can only be experienced and understood in the present. What happens to us within is what we are acquainted with and experience in the outer world.

When your mind is at peace, you did not hear any noise. If you do not hear any noise, then there is only peace emerging in your mind. Peace is between the noise and the silence. If you are able to feel a complete silence all outside noises will have no effect on you.

This is because you do not hear any in the mind. It is a wonderful and peaceful feeling when you have reached the emptiness level in your mind. You can choose what to hear and what not to. When your mind is void a true peace will emerge. A true peace is you aligned with "**The Source**" and have a tremendous uplift feeling of self-control, self-esteem, and confidence to achieve your goals and desires. Your direction is clear and thoughtful. The abilities to manifest peace and love depend on the ability to recognize the inner energy dwelling in you and this truth is extended to the outer state of consciousness. You see radical new ideas change your belief system and reshape your vision to see a new outcome. Your thoughts are more lucid and tranquil allowing your true state to engage a peaceful and loving approach to life. All these opposite feelings are being replaced with compassion and kindness. As your thought patterns have changed and a better life will follow. The result is that you build strength through the same subjective mind to eliminate failure and discomfort, while letting your peaceful mind takeover.

Finally, when your mind is at peace there is nothing from the outside force can irritate and displease you. You have your house in order and the mind is your obedient servant and peaceful ally. Your mind will not bring anything to displease you and thought will automatically filter before it enters into the conscious mind. Since your thoughts are guiding you, you no longer are affected by your pervious disharmony thoughts rushing into your mind without invitation. For this reason you have changed your conscious thoughts and changed your destiny.

The more we depend upon the subconscious mind and the power of our loving mind; we will find ourselves bestowed with many amazing blessings and the miracle of living truly.

Chapter Six
~Consciousness—CONSCIENCE, Awareness, Karma and **The Source**~

Is it true that people with no conscience have no soul? What make them do what they do to others? I heard people saying you have done so many evil things to hurt others in your life don't you have a conscience? Do you have a soul? I don't think conscience is in their minds otherwise they would not have done it. I wonder where these people went after they pass on. People, who scam, con, cheat for a living; they are predators. I always believe people are aware of what they do. Many of you have seen this movie "The Red Dragon" a true story. The movie describes very well this person, who is a massive killer, believes himself is a devil from hell, loves to kill humans with cold blood, and drinks their bloods. Everything happened for a reason. The cause of his action is due to unstoppable hatred in his mind and bloods, which drove him to do evil things to release his hatred and continue to kill in cold blood. However, doctors diagnose this insanity as psychologically in balance and perhaps have temporal damages in their brains. It also can be affected by mood swings that cause them to do knowingly or unknowingly.

Where do these people go after they die? If hell is created to balance the difference between good and evil or heaven and hell. Then, hell does exist to balance what is absent to make men feel more comfortable in their minds. It is widely held belief that if people do evil things their souls will go to "?"

Again, this warns people if you do evil activities towards others your

90

soul will migrant to hell in the later day. However, there are people still doing things to hurt others because of their greed and envy. A better explanation is the balance of the nature.

People, who have superb conscience, will do humanitarian acts to each other. They have a fabulous heart. In their hearts and souls, they simply love people for example, Princess Diana. She is the Queen of Hearts in Heaven now. They love children, people, and animals, because of their selflessness. Mother Teresa loves to do humanitarian work for the moral goodness of mankind and she was a great humanitarian. These loving, caring, compassionate people have benevolent qualities in their hearts and are sent directly from God to help humans to improve life on Earth. It is incredible to have them around. They make you feel great, joyful, and full of peace. The word of *conscience is defined as the consciousness connected to moral goodness or blameworthiness in one's own conduct, intentions, or character together with a feeling of obligation to do right or be good. (*Merriam-Webster)

The common usage in which the term "consciousness" is synonymous with "awareness" or "*conscious awareness.*" It connects us generally with, such as thoughts, feelings, images, dreams, and body experiences and so on, but also the experience of the three-dimensional world (the physical world) beyond the body surface. It is important to distinguish between consciousness and awareness. Awareness means having knowledge of something because you have observed it or somebody has told you about it.

For instance, when you meet someone you know on the street, your brain does not need to scan through your old memory to recognize your old friend. It recognizes it automatically or instantly, at a deeper level of *awareness.*

While *consciousness* means being awake and aware of surroundings. The state of being awaken is the awareness of what happens in the environment surrounding you. Through our mind and thoughts for example, a thought connects with another person's consciousness enabling to be opened to communication. One man was worrying about his dying Dad. He looked up at the sunset and saw his face in his mind, while his voice distinctly said, "forgive me." A few hours later that man called his brother in Seattle, he discovers that he had the same vision and heard the same words.

Clarity about consciousness is vitally important. If we cannot properly name something, we do not know it. In addition, we have no knowledge of it; we have no influence over it.

When we reach a period in our human evolvement and expansion in our consciousness and are then reflected in our world if we are to live a meaningful and purposeful life. Meaning and purpose are the primary fruits of consciousness development.

Consciousness is what forms, what it is. It is defined as a person who reaches for enlightenment. It is the substantial essence of things, which uncovers its universal truth and its singular individual characteristics. Consciousness is the soul of many possible realities and is its essence.

Everyone has a soul and everyone is aware of its potential. Each person or thing is a distinct individual. However, we are all part of something larger than ourselves. It is consciousness or soul, which binds us to our larger universal nature, sometimes called the divine oneness.

When you are conscious, you employ your heart, your intuition, or your faculties of knowing to expand the mind, and other teaching bodies that exist in the realm of the soul. Thus, when you are aware of your conscience, you are not separated from what you know. You then merge with it. You identify with it as you test it. It moves with you in a manner that you test it as a part of your larger individuality.

When you are aware, you employ your mind to recognize something in an objective way. You know more about something. You have the knowledge, but you know you are separated from the thing you know. Awareness occurs, as mental reflex, at any time, when the mind is exposed to something, the only choice is concentrating on the truth and advances our knowledge.

You could call the conscious 'heart of knowing.' The beauty of the heart knows it is not separated from what it knows or meets. It is seen another way. By fully knowing, we are touched by its essence and in this manner; we resemble what we know. Because of soul beings, we are primarily love.

Through this knowing the soul, we develop and increase our sense of direction of who we are as infinite beings. We find peace and harmony in our relationship with people and situations, and we approach a deeper consciousness.

No men are more powerful than others, except **The Source** and the power in you. No race is supreme than others. In the beginning, God created men equally. The supremacist idealist is not guided by self consciousness and to think so is very idiotic and unacceptable. It is an old belief or an idea created in the past with an intention to control or degrade others.

Karma is fair to everyone especially when wronged and Karma will get back to you. Every action there is a reaction. Each existence is caused by the first and followed by the second event and arises either pleasant or unpleasant. Another way of explaining Karma is the law of cause and effect. A person action bounces and flows back to him.

If the action caused is unpleasantness, the effect is a huge damage, painful financial lost because of his action, and the consequences will return to the root. Even though, seemingly it might not have happened immediately, but definitely it will return to him. Every action is recorded in each individual's data sheet. You are responsible for your own reckless action towards other people. No one can escape one's action. It is like an express train has arrived in front of you, already on the platform without any prior warning.

When you realize its arrival is too late, and there is no negotiation with your own karma, it will haunt you and until your paid. God is watching over all your action. Remember every one of your actions will bounce back, but there is always a hint that the Divine is watching.

When you feel that you have been touch by grace, which is your hint that God is around you and cares about what happens to you. When a robber committed criminal acts, as a result he is arrested and sentence to prison, which is his karma that befalls on him, due to his own cause and effect. Grace could happen in any form if the robber changed his mind and quit the robbery that would have changed his destiny.

What comes around goes around. So, how does karma repayment work?

Karma emerges without forewarning, however, it is directed by the *Divine Light Power*. It approaches you in an extreme speed and you are not even aware of it. It is "*unavoidable* and *inescapable*." When you are in the center of a Karmic situation, you feel unclear, and perhaps you feel strangely incapable of breaking away from the situation. You are shocked at how this occurred to you, without warning.

When you are in the center of a Karmic situation, you feel unclear, and perhaps you feel strangely incapable of breaking away from the situation. You are shocked at how this occurred to you, without warning. You are unconsciously driven into a difficult and perplex situation.

The complete event and situation is like a dream, but it is real. In the situation, you will meet with some people, but unknown to you they are your nightmare and karmic debts. These people emerge to claim your karmic debts. You are a sleeper in the train. Until the experiences and prices of your pervious inappropriate action has been paid in full. **You are not able to awaken.** Your protective armor has been removed temporarily. You're aware of something wrong, but too weaken to withdraw yourself from the situation. In other words, you are not able to unlock yourself from that unwanted situation until the end is near. Then, slowly you regain your consciousness and begin to awaken.

The karma can last as long as seven years for paying back for your improper actions towards others. It has a long lasting effect on your improper action, so think deeply before you act and act accordingly.

The reason for Karma ending is for you to be unbiased on the matter so that you can evolve to a new level. You have achieved the neutral position in the triadic experience and you are ready for something different. Balance is the name of the game. However, in order for karma to be truly paid off, the parties involved must acknowledge the completion of it, at this level. As the Karma piles up and becomes more intense, lifetime after lifetime, until eventually the lesson of forgiveness is learned. Illness is part of our karma, and is important for people to experience their karma, their destiny, and their bitterness, or sweet or bittersweet gifts from the Universe. If you could see beyond the illusion realm of the subjective experience, your body is suffering, but you are not.

Certainly good karma will replace the old karma. The same will apply, if you do something unwise, you will expect a rocky returns. If you pray for everybody during your silent connection with the Divine, you have created a good deed to yourself, but also transform good energy to everyone and benefit the whole Universe. Eventually, it will have a profound impact on your life and also on everyone around you.

The Universe is the body of the invisible Source known as God. The omnipresence of God is everywhere. Space fills with trillions of stars in the outer space, and is full of mystery of mysterious, which created by an invisible *Mind of God* of *Universal Creative Life Energy*.

Every living creature including the rain forests and the beautiful flowers are the art works of God. Therefore, God fills the *Universe* in all its part and is present everywhere.

Sir Isaac Newton believed that the Universe was literally God's blank mind and all of the stars and galaxies were His thoughts. God has no shape and *He* is limitless. He lives in an empty space in the fifth dimension and with limitless source. God is beyond time and space. It is difficult for humans to understand God creations. To reach God by quietly listening to the inner voice in us and feel *His* omnipresence and power.

Again, every desire leads to an action and it gives rise to an outcome. When you pray to God and convey to Him what you need and you will receive a response from *Him*.

You will be guided and told how to move towards that direction to reach your desires so that you know what it is you ask for is answered, but you have to stretch your boundaries a little bit to get results.

HERMAN WONG

Through prayer, we express our feeling of joy and happiness, challenges and difficulties to the Divine every day. Our desires and thoughts flow through the *Universe* and all our prayers return to us answered. Even if it is not answered at this moment, it will be answered in *His* time. You confess that you have the answer by keeping the faith and it is all yours.

Remember, having complete faith and believing in God is supporting you to fill all your needs. If your desire does not come true, after a while be patient and continue to have faith, and claim your victory over all difficulties and despairs. When your faith is not depended on just getting an answer, but trust in God, then suddenly, you realize you have received all glory that awaits you.

Life is full of challenges. If life has no challenges it would be unproductive and non-constructive because there is no decision or desire filling this void in life, we need to look for the positive. It helps to heal any situation at hand. It reminds me that in every storm there is a chance of rainbow that will break into the sky and find happiness in my heart, nourish my soul and lifts my spirit. Even in the midst of suffering, you still can break through into consciousness and be free from pain. It is in the realm of spirit that heals our hearts.

Let the situation unfold to blossom, but stay in an active side instead of passive. The decision is in your hands, you can turn catastrophe into triumph and considered all the blessings of God is answered now.

Holding and repeating thoughts and transcending them into a void space of the Universe will transform your dreams into physical reality. Your thoughts are a powerful energy. It materializes your wishes and desires to form from formless, and returns to you with a positive outcome. You need to be grateful for everything that you achieve and witness your ultimate success. You give thanks to God grace, the Universes invisible resources, and the people who are involve with you along the way and yourself to be aware of this desire and the idea becomes known.

Living life to the fullness is one of the challenges in creating greater

96

success in your life. When you can live life to the fullness, it would be the greatest joy you have ever given to yourself. Then, you live with joy and blissfulness.

Five virtual deeds you must do before you complete your journey on Earth.

First, you ought to forgive yourself and others. You know it is impossible to change the past, but you can change the relationships you have with yourself and in yourself. You can let go of certain events in your life by just releasing it. You must be aware that you are releasing the past condition that seems to repeat itself and this old condition cannot be released until you are ready.

It is a thought however, that you can release this inner guilt captivating you and your inability to forgive yourself. You can clear the past by recreating what you did and allowing yourself to forgive and let go of any resentment and attachment you have to them. By eliminating old thoughts you move towards new thoughts and understanding of yourself and a stronger alignment with your *Inner Source*. Your willingness to forgive is not holding onto the past again. Immediately, you have empowered the will of forgiveness to let your mind be free of old thoughts and believe you have no intention of revisiting again!

Next, you affirm that you have forgiven yourself and the person who had misused your trust in the past. The painful past is no longer an issue and you are ready to move on to live a truly joyful life. You continue to transform your thought vibrations towards your *Source* energy.

Then, you begin to reconcile your life and infuse it with love and peace. You allow yourself to open to a new consciousness and penetrate deep into your mind and have faith in the progress to go forward and live the life that you envision.

This does not need to be a lengthily process to manifest your life and can occur instantaneously. The moment you have decided on abundance in your life will depend on the quality of energy and intention. We are our own enemies, if something is not manifested correctly, we will always know the roots of the problem.

After, starting a new habit you will see better results than you did in the past. Keep in mind a strong emotion, detachment and patience will create any desired result.

Finally, you realize that your patient and faith are needed to achieve a better flow in your life and you will have the control that your desire. Practice meditation periodically will help you to feel the inner peace. Now you believe that life offers gift of joy and only God can give that power to you. You realize God is powerful and *His* love is there for you.

Therefore, the conclusion is you believe your life is no longer living in a strange dream. You begin to appreciate life and eliminate every problem on your plate, so you will not repeat them. The blunders you have amended give you an opportunity to transform negative thoughts to positive energy on a daily basis. Eliminate any doubtful thoughts that you still process, and infuse them with positive intention for a personal transformation. This will do well and opportunities are always open to you for your evaluation and a better understand of self.

The opportunity is always there for you to make that leap—waiting for you to perceive your weakness and make an internal and external transformation. *It does not matter what happened in the past and you alone can make that transformation and begin to live in the Now.* It is for your own personal development and spiritual evolution. Nobody can give it to you but yourself.

It opens a channel to new thoughts and conceptual ideas. Once the situations improve, you will be a winner.

Then, you will grow freely. Mistakes have motivated us to change our negative thoughts into positive actions. Such ideas or thoughts will help us to reconsider our motives to direct us to the right path and change our attitude towards self to become aware of what is important in our lives.

"The ancient Indian described a great joy and paralyzing fear as two strong and fertile soils that penetrate from the world of illusion into a high mindfulness."

Roosevelt said, "The only thing we have to fear is fear itself."

If you can overcome fear, everything will turn around in your favor. With that said, you shift your focus to success and you will find that fear will begin to fade away and be replaced with more abundance that you can enjoy in your life. You are not escaping from your fear, but you replace them with trust and faith, and create your own self-consciousness. Once you have created your awareness you know how to deal with it. The problem in front of you is not a challenge, but a joyful event.

Experience tells us when a lesson is learned we no longer need that lesson. Then, we move on to the next level. When all the lessons are learned peace remains and your Karma is complete.

This is not an absolution from God, but is a lesson in learning the truth about yourself and is for your spiritual growth.

Chapter Seven
~Free Thought…~

You find inner-peace when you are enjoying everything you do with a positive mental attitude. When you create a powerful relationship with yourself, you trigger a specific response in your heart with joy and happiness. There are people who work with a truthful and passionate attitude in the work they do. They believe everything is alive, because of that attitude they have more energy and feel the joy in their hearts. In fact, whatever you do is a reflection. It reflects your personalities, thoughts and feelings, and attitude towards what you believe from within and connects to the real work that you do in the outer environment. It is an action of your choice to match with your Inner Source and mirrors inner image, and your imagination is your connecting link to the external world. So, if you match this inner speech with your external experiences and you will be respected and recognized by others and these steadfast actions and contributions, you have executed will ultimately be realized.

Some people view life like a show, a dance, but it mirrors what we believe. How you act shows a reflection of how we will respond in our realistic world. Imagine what you do is now being recognized by others.

It is because of your passion, integrity and a positive attitude allows the inner completion to be expressed and you are focused on an image that there is never lacking a Universal supply and how it will all come into sight. You believe that the Universal Mind will always provide you with every blessing in abundance. Your thought on abundance will automatically radiate this energy and transcends it to the Universe and ultimately, it becomes your inner truth.

Nothing can prevent you from materialize your dreams and desire into reality. This is true because anything you focus on for a substantial period will trigger and be supported by the *Law of Magnetic* energy to translate your dream into physical equivalent.

When you focus on an idea or thought long, enough it will activate the magnetic energy of the invisible Universe's frequency to resonate with you contemplate on and is return to you. You can write down a list of your desires on paper with exact details and begin focusing and meditating on it until it becomes a true reality. The more time you spend on meditate on a particular subject in the subliminal mind you have added more power and energy in it. It also triggers the vibrational thought energy towards the higher intentional field and raises the energy to the outer limits.

By shifting a positive mental attitude you resonate with your Source and continue feeling bliss within, and know that your energy is now reached to the highest peak, gaining growth and momentum through your awareness and with everything on track, you know your higher vibrational energy is matched up with the force of creation and reflects the desires and your trueness in your life.

When an artist prints his art, he infuses it with love and passion. Enthusiasm is the main motivation to his success. He filled his art with genuine feelings, thoughts, and vibrations. The artwork is alive and reflects his actual genius and experience. Consequently, he is able to generate income and attract positive energy to realize his hopes and desires. When you add truthfulness and enthusiasm in your work it reflects and improves the quality of everything tremendously. It is faith inspires you to do the best.

The best way to realize your dreams is to meditate in silence, because through meditation you are in thoughtless awareness, then this development of awareness occurs. In your conscious state, you can write down a list of preferences to help you to see how you want your desires to express to them. You can write down positive and negative desires. If you are in alignment with your desire, you know precisely what you have chosen and it reaches the apex on your list. However, if your preference is not on the list, then you can add it. It is a good idea for you to read it aloud so that you can hear the vibration of the words echo back to you.

Then, you know you have intuitively connected to the one particular thought that appeals to you. It helps tapping into the silence to hear and feel the vibration of those words and immediately you have your choice. As soon as you acknowledge your choice you can transform your objective into action and with faith your dream will become factual.

Here is something that is very interesting from my experience.

I closed my eyes, meditate on the silence, and in my mind's eye a vision of scene emerge to me. I feel complete silence in my mind. I see an ocean of space appearing in its depths of darkness and something emerges in front me. It is far off in a distance as it rotates 360-degrees and it explodes before me at a fantastic speed like a rising sun on the horizon, I am mesmerized and pulled towards it, I can feel the hotness of its light, suddenly, it transforms into a virtual image of a huge portal. I penetrated into this portal and saw another portal opening one after another. They are embedded with seven vivid colors and there are seven portals. The last portal is neon gold.

I unlocked it with a key. I turned the knob to enter into the portal through a curtain of gold light. I was shocked at what I saw. I viewed a hologram image standing on the podium talking to a huge audience. The message he was talking about sounded familiar to me. I looked up and there was a huge banner hanging across the platform "**The Awareness of Magnetic Energy.**"

Hey, I know what you are talking about it is my idea, I thought. This idea has not yet been published. As soon as, I thought, my spiritual visions faded away I was awakening to the present. Then, in that instant, I awoke. However, I still felt the present of the bright gold light and held its power over my body. All of sudden, I realize that this book has already transcended into the Universe and is a reality. I feel it shows me in my conscious states I am not aware of everything, but only in an unconscious state of mind, do I know the events have happened. I can tap into this experience of higher consciousness in my infinite self and feel inner joy and happiness. Through soul meditation, creative visualization, and alignment with **The Source**, I come to a realization that **The Source** has granted my desire. I accept my desire is real and the *Universe* responds in the same manner.

I realize in my experience in life is beyond a physical body, we are connected with an infinite soul. Because you are an infinite soul, it allows you to see beyond your own reality, time, and space to recognize the inner truth is within. This recognition enables you to realize there is no fear, worry, or scarcity and is just an illusion. As soon as, you eliminate this idea of struggling you carry more energies and strengths. Indeed, we only use 4% of the Universal supply therefore, trust your *Inner Knowing* will move you to a fertile ground and to a peaceful place so that you can create your desire intention and feel the creativity, kindness, love, abundance and anything that you desire that's consistence with the *Universal Mind* and will come together for you.

When I am thinking of a person I thought of the restful energy that this person has brought me. I thought of the joyful and happy events recorded in my subconscious mind. Immediately, I feel inner peace flowing into my spirit gaining insight and certainty of truthfulness. I was more reassured that the inner part of me is intuitive, wise and perfectly resonate with my heart. The *Inner Source* provides a new knowledge based upon things that can't be obtained from the external consciousness. The *Inner Knowing* continues to guide my soul journey and nothing can impede me. I am exuberant and I can't wait to find out what comes next in the unfolding of my soul's drama.

Everything happened for a reason and everything does happen for the best. Everything happened is God will and then your will is realized. I believe it is important to pay attention to the messages or signs that the external world is trying to communicate and understand this is actually the symbol for the inner events. In other words, the inner event was the plan that I wanted to save. The Invisible mind has a plan behind how everything will happen in the outer world. If the events do not happen right away, I do not jump to a conclusion and believe it will come as a surprise. I do not run out of patience, but instead of letting my mind be confused by many different angles of thinking, I remain calm in the inner state of mind and do not need outside validation.

God-realization is a direct personal feeling of God within oneself. It is an individual experience and belief that God is consciously present in their hearts. It is an infinite energy you won't find anywhere.

You realize that you want to join yourself with this unique and powerful entity; you want to understand it; you want to explore, control, and use it. God-realization can be experienced through the individual mind, therefore everyone experiences this differently. The latent subconscious mind recognizes God infinite energy in them at the time of true connection and then feels the joy, happiness, and tranquility flowing through them. God-realization is an individual experience and is a declaration of his own recognition and realization of the hidden beauty of the mind and its infinite reality. It frees the conscious mind from the ego, and the power is beyond the limitation of the mental mind. The awareness of God brings the realization the soul knows of its connection to the infinite reality. The soul is awakening to the infinite knowledge of itself, because the soul then realizes that this suppression has separated it from its source. The limitless of aptitude is restored by infinite awakening and the restlessness of experiences is reinstated by peace.

You are awakened by the invisible *Source* that urges you to discover your own truth. The inner world has little activity. You do not know where to look for an answer unless you have seen the light from within, but God has left no footprint or visible clue in the material world. So you rest and wait. When you stop thinking, then an answer arises to surprise you. Strangely, wisdom arrives only when you quiet the mind and still your thoughts. It is logical when the mind is silent, thoughtlessness, and calm, you realize the peace of the infinite reality.

When the mind is silent, the infinite mind can take over to

acknowledge any answer coming forth with. But, while the mind is interrupted by the battling of the mental mind this will block the real answer to reaching your mind. Peace consciousness helps you to tap into the inner silence for knowledge, wisdoms, aptitudes, miracles and transform everything seemingly impossible to become a reality of your choice.

You realize at the end of a spiritual journey you return to God. But, before you can reach back to God you must understand at each stage, God has guided you on a spiritual journey where the end is clear and total peace, therefore, nothing will cause fear to you.

Your mission is not to configure how fates are unfolding. You are here to refine the soul on Earth. You are here to learn spiritual lessons until the whole journey is completed. Every event happened has cosmic order and random events are guided by the invisible *Source*. Reality changes at different stages of growth. Chaos may just be an illusion and there is a total order for all events because of the power of divinity. Every uncertain event can be answered by the *Inner Knowing*. A wise man feels inner calm and tranquility and he does not panic. He understands the ups and downs of this condition shall pass and peace will prevail.

Your soul journey is inspired and guided by inner passion and can be self-fulfilled. Your self-acceptance becomes the way to God.

You have blissfully accepted you are an infinite being. When your inner soul is detached from the body it is the time you shall meet God. It may be a bit cold hearted, but you no longer need to distinguish between God and you or you and God, but are simply one source.

However, while you still living on Earth your soul journey is guided by inner passion and demands its own fulfillment. Your soul fulfillment is to learn many lessons and complete your journey on Earth. God is silently guiding and watching over your life. Your actions today define your future. All past actions have a way of mirroring the future effects. But, good deeds and thoughts are a reflection of tomorrow. Nevertheless, events happen, because you must experience those lessons and there is no short cut.

The good news is you won't be asked to repeat that lesson, because it is unnecessary. All events must occur for you to gain experience with them and grow towards peace.

It is faith that put you closer to God. It is love, which detaches you from improper conduct. You accept things as they are. You act accordingly to the *Inner Voice* urgings and you take it easy on yourself. It is so important that you are being yourself and connected to the invisible source of the Universal flow of life.

Life will continue to create and be recreated through the *Universal Mind of Creative Life Force*. The infinite power of God has no beginning and no ending. God's energy will light your feelings, thoughts, intelligence, and reality and is extending forever.

You have done a lot of inner work to remove self-doubt and disbeliefs about one's imperfection. You know that your intentions count. Many positive events have happened as a result of feeling bliss and peacefulness. All because you have faith in God and God is assisting your creative events.

Faith and belief gives you hope and expectation to experience life in its fullness. Since you do not know how your spiritual journey has been mapped out, deciding good or bad should not be left to your ego. The ego hates uncertainty, but on the road to explore life there are periods of uncertainty and even lack of safety. Therefore, the challenge is to align with your Sources intention for you—God's will.

You are free to accept or reject God realization from within. When you are consciously connected with the Source you have accepted the truth and the truth will liberate you. Now you have recreated a relationship with the *Universal Mind*.

You are realigned with **The Source**, because you were not conscious of creation. The external events have confused or flawed your ideas because you believed you are separated from **The Source**.

The truth is you have never been separated from **The Source**. But, now you recognize **The Source** energy is always dwelling in you and your soul feels with the bliss and tranquility.

You can ask questions to the mind and wait for an answer to arrive. As soon as you start approaching the invisible *Source* and unbelievable expression of self emerges and there is no other explanation of this incredible power. Then, the answer is self explanatory.

You have secured your soul connection with **The Source** and you are living in the Now. You are no longer living in fear or being a vessel for negative emotions and that bliss and peace has filled your infinite soul. You have no negative influences in the mind, but contentment. You are more intuitive with everything you do, because your soul is feeling cheerful and peaceful. You have inner visions of clarity about your life.

You have loved **The Source** since connection, and seen the beauty of it and the loveliness of the bountiful *Universe*. Now you acknowledge **The Sources** power has always been manifested from within and projected by you to the external world.

The mission of peaceful *Universe* is possible, if each individual is at peace with each self. Your peaceful intention and positive vibrational thoughts will touch the heart of others through the energy of collective consciousness to bring peace.

Imagine the world is at peace and is infused with God's love. If everyone is focusing on a single vision in their mind for peace, then someday there will be peace on Earth. This will happen through the collective consciousness of soul's connection and consciously align with the *Universal Mind*, to bring peace, abundance, joy, and happiness, and then peaceful desire will be transformed. Every being on this planet is a partner and co-creator therefore, it is possible that this vision of global initiative for peace can continue to evolve and progress, and some day when it is strong, enough it will transform into reality, and make God's peace on Earth, a reality.

Chapter Eight
~LOVE Consciousness~

Everything you do is a reflection of love and it brings success to your venture. Using the power of love to influence the planetary position will bring the veracity of love to all. Love bonds the world together. It is love awareness that understand we live peacefully on Earth.

A person success is what he does, because he is enthusiastic and loves to succeed. His successes are sustained by the energy of love and the keenness contributing to his work and joys. He is always looking forward to the next business day, because he loves to work. Business associate value his business, because of his positive attitude and blissful vibrations that he brings to them. You are acknowledged in your business, because you have infused the enthusiasm of love into what you do.

Perhaps you have received help by a mentor earlier; therefore, the influential energy you collected is now transcended back into your business with the power of liveliness. Love has shinned on your heart and you are selfless. Love consciousness expands by itself although you may not notice this energy and the presence of the conditions of love, but it is like an *"old oak tree growing stronger, and strengthened and gradually its energy transcend to within the one."*

By giving your love and heart to others, you have opened the channels of loves energy to flow through to others. When your heart is opened to give love, your love quickly slips through time and space and activates a direct link between the two of you. That links is always there. It is there, because everything is manifested and connected with love.

Being conscious of love is easier for your spiritual growth. It is love, when you have a deep connection to everything and is always activated. The love vibrations that you send have no boundary or boarder; therefore it will be received by all. It is love encompasses everything that exists and nothing can be created without the unified field of Loves power.

In your heart, the world is one living place and others are free to receive any love energy transcending to them. It is because you believe there is no partiality or restriction in God's love. Therefore, you should be able to extend God's love and consciously transcend peace to planet Earth. We use love to balance the nature and neutralize the negative influences. As soon as we begin the process of bringing balance back to Earth with God's love, then the world will be one peaceful place.

Everything you do is motivated by two invisible powerful forces: the *power of peace* and the power *of love*. Without these two energies, nothing can be created and triggered. Love connects every human to each other. God created this Earth with the energy of "Love" and "Peace." We are the creation of God's love and we are created to receive that "Love." Life is *"for giving"* love to all. Giving love to other is forgiveness. The two words *"forgive"* can form together into one word "forgiveness"

When we forgive, and forget and love ourselves and we have forgotten our blunders. Therefore, love is a key word in expressing forgiveness to others. When love is present we have transformed our thoughts to positive energy, and experienced the spirit of love and transcend this to the *Universe*. *"Love is to all. Light is to all. Truth is to all."*

When you feel pain for a period, I believe you will look for release from those intolerable pains. RIGHT! As soon as you have awakened to God's consciousness I believe your pains will reduce to a minimum. It sounds unbelievable, but it can be validated. It is God's love that gives life to you and me; therefore it is absolutely dependable and trustable. It is love consciousness that allow you to let go of control and believe that the invisible power of God will take care of these pains. You do not need to struggle with the pains alone, but replace them with love and forgiveness. You forgive yourself for experiencing the pains infused into your body. This is because disease or illness occurs due to lack of care of yourself and warn you to love yourself. Sooner you realize this and start to love yourself and the pains will reduce to minimum or zero. You can "*ADD*" a healthy nutrition to your diet for your physical being and the soul will appreciate you.

When you provide material supplies to help others to meet their end needs you do it for the consciousness of love? You are kind; because you perceive and fill with God's love in everything, you see and do. Your heart is filled with love energy and you are enthusiastic about how you help others, because you are a true believer and devotee to God.

You give blessing to everything you see, and touch, and even to an empty space. You enjoy doing this, because you believe everything is infused with liveliness and can be seen or unseen, and they fit into this category of God's love and peace.

When you recognize God-Consciousness, sometime the awareness is either coming from a prophetic word or through your active action. During a conversation with someone there, words inspire you and touch you. This has ignited your inner attention and suddenly you feel God has spoken to you through the wisdom of this person. This happens because God's is omnipresent is everywhere and is intelligent for what *He* does.

When your inner awareness is not yet activated you can't respond to your inner needs without being directed or guided by others. .

I remembered 5 years ago I had this conversation with a friend. Suddenly, I felt my inner energy was triggered by the words used within that conversation. I recognize the significant of these words "...the manifestation of unlimited bliss and tranquility in consciousness and you know...it's ah, *soul-enrichment*...and this latent ability of infinite reality" Immediately, was transformed because I knew these words contain the knowledge of my essence and I have been inspired by them to do my soul searching. Immediately, I am aware of something that has just been activated. In fact, my inner system has just been awakened by the invisible hands of God.

These words continuously to have a profound effect on my life and it has triggered and connected me with **The Source**. Now I have understood my inner needs are in alignment with **The Source** and I have accepted myself and others. From that moment onward God has opened my heart to spiritual awareness. After the spiritual realization I continue to go deeper within to find more insight regarding my being. I am now conscious of how important it is to connect with God that enables me to embrace everything with God's love.

Miracles happen to you every day, love, health, wealth, and success can be obtained, but you must know how to transform them into your life. You know it can be seen with your own eyes, but you can also get help from the spirit in your heart. It is the sacred place where you look for help for anything you desire to be, to do and to have effectively. Knowledge and wisdoms can be obtained through meditation and the conscious power of your *Inner Self*. There are no limits with regards to how you can utilize these powers. They are receptive to you and unreserved, but you must ask and it is given. These tools will awaken your full potential. The *Inner Source* will open your heart to give and receive love. The joy of truly being aware of your desires is a conscious connection to self and with your *Source* and is a sense of recognizing your purpose to continue to develop and grow.

There are different levels of love, but one main aspect of this is to give love to others and receiving love back. If you fall in love with someone or others will fall in love with you. It is true in a sense. But it is not necessary. This is because you love her for who she truly is.

However, if you choose to send love to someone you truly love; you can always send her love and the heartfelt power of God's light. You probably will receive an echo back from her. Her infinite soul will respond to your subconscious signal and will whisper back to you "I received your love and accepted your heart and thank you." This is true! We are connected with one collective power of consciousness. We are created in the image of God and God is "LOVE" therefore, we are love. I believe if you desire to receive love and your Inner Source known you are seeking for love and will bring the loves energy to you.

We don't have to plan for a new thought, but simply generate love for everything and then all things will manifest to us. Love is the basic foundation in creation and love is the solution. Love will neutralize the ignorance of others, their prejudice, misunderstanding, or judgments. Indeed, to resolve these problems all you need is your intention of being open to your heart and release your problems, argument, or any outstanding issue that you are facing, give it a thought and pause for a moment, then apply loves energy to the roots of these problems. If your love energy is strong enough it will expose the truth, and the problems will be resolved shortly. You will know when a solution emerges to you. You will experience *ah ha* feelings from within. You know you have just cracked an egg shell to resolve your dilemma.

Again, if you want love you must experience it for yourself and no one can give this experience to you.

(*For example, my only nephew, who has obtained two degrees with a distinct honor in Economics and Law in 2008, had spent a full month travelling across Europe. He has gained an incredible life experiences to add onto his uniqueness and resume. While in Europe he had learned to take care of himself and gained more experiences, while interacting with other cultures. With enthusiasm, love and passion he had completed a journey across Europe successfully. It is no doubt in my mind he has learned and benefited from this trip in the best of ways and has helped with his development. He has also revealed the power of love to others and himself. He exposed the truth of his intention. He showed his determination to succeed, demonstrated love to others and himself through this invaluable trip. With love's qualities that he has, there is the potential for greater relationship to develop. Therefore, I believe God's love continues shinning on him for further successes and beyond.*)*

Each human is unique and special. We have different talents, aptitudes, appearances, faith, and beliefs. While expressing difference in cultures and ideas it is love that illustrates that life is all in one. The one energy is the same infinite qualities of the love of the Mind of God. God is love and everyone will agree upon this, and is the basic truth and no one can deny this power.

"There is no substitute for love."
BURCE BARTON 1953

Chapter Nine
~Problem Solving~

When you desire to live a spiritual life, it does not mean that you are immune from any problems arising in your life. But, it means that you aware of your *Inner Source* and will navigate you to live a quiet creative life. You feel inner quietness and tranquility from within, because your life has completely transformed in a more receptive and productive way. Since you are connected with the *Inner Source*, you realize life has changed and progressed, because this is the life you deliberately chose to live. It leads everything and becomes more visible and obvious, but not confused or complicated. You released all suppressions in your past to give way to new thoughts and this allow your ability to link from within and you are no longer feeling bound to any earthy attachments. You love yourself, because of knowing *self*-love is important and this attribute of your character, which allows you to recognize you are an infinite being. Your calm attitude is always reflected on your face and expressed to the outer state of consciousness. You experience the world in its fullness, because you feel God's omnipresence and its energy.

The *Inner Knowing* will silently navigate and advise you on important issues. Through meditation from within you will hear the *Inner Voice* guiding you silently and connect to your insight, knowledge, and wisdom and to generate these skills to resolve any difficult situations quickly and steadfastly.

However, during meditation you may ask **The Source** to reveal any standing problems that you may have in your life. To hear the *Inner Silence* respond and speak to you in a soft voice, you must lucid your mind to hear this. Because, when the mind is silent, it is blissful and there is no clutter thought, you can hear and receive advice clearly to resolve your problems in the flexible world. You resonate with harmony and peace, and realize the omnipresence of God. The peaceful and relaxing mind is the essence of everyone's desires and can be attained by meditating on the dim light from within. Sooner, you achieve the stages of inner peace and blissful happiness and you will eliminate all your stresses, anxieties, worries, fears, mental restlessness, and being impatient. It is a state of inner serenity and tranquility, which brings you this harmonious state of joys and gratifications, give you the ability to endure the hardship and difficulty and helps to create inner balance and self-control and that gives rise to contentment.

However, if you want to achieve deeper inner state of peace, to overcome your everyday problems, then you have to spend more time practicing meditation on love, compassion, and benevolence.

Because, when you meditate on inner peace through the fist of faith it establishes a mutual relationship with **The Source** and gain self-assurance and strengthens a positive mental attitude in your outlook in life.

On the spiritual level you learn to listen to God response to you. Sooner, you will recognize each level is a stepping stone that guides your walk to the right spiritual path towards the light. The longer you practice meditation on **The Source** your mental attitude will improve and transform. You will have more positive ways of thinking, building more endurance overtime and a better connection to our conscious your thoughts and you will gain appreciation for life. Therefore, you won't engage in meaningless activities.

When you meditate deeper on the inner self to eliminate self-destructive thoughts about human suffering and let God release and join in *His* liberation and "*Nirvana*" this can be attained by joining your heart and mind to God, and then you reach the tranquility of spiritual calmness and inner peace. Gradually, you realize life is too precious to waste on being offended easily by people's words, feelings, and behaviors. You open yourself to Divine's flow and the energy of love and you are so happy that you have joined this part of self that has brought you perfect health and vitality. You just say aloud, "**oh, yes it is joy and fun to be alive.**" When you open yourself and invite the infinite Source *He* will welcome you.

When the infinite comes to you, remember *He* will keep you in *His* loving thought, embrace you, and administer *His* love and guidance. Keep your door open and your heart close to God to hear *Him* so that He may enter your mind.

In reality, to resolve a problem you must be detached from the problem first, then meditated the answers from within and recognize the problems can be resolved in due time. It is as if you want to delete a file in a Hard Drive of your computer, you must delete the sub-folder first, and then you can delete the main directory. You can't delete the directory prior deleting the subfolder. It won't let you do it. It is that simple and now you know.

The operations of the mind are operated by two different modes: the subconscious mind and the conscious mind. You must be aware that the latent subconscious mind is the *Inner Knowing* and to possess this powerful resource, knowledge, and wisdom, you must resonate with it. However, on the mental level it is the conscious mind giving command to the subconscious to transform your dreams into action in the physical world. The conscious mind is the subjective mind directs you to every external event in the world, because it is connected to the external environment; therefore it is easily filled with clutter and negative energy that affects your decision and judgment.

But, the mental mind has the ability to develop a higher degree of understanding to perceive a better image and use of the power of reasoning by impressing upon the subconscious mind to carry the desired command by you. Thus, the conscious mind becomes the guardian of the subconscious mind.

The subconscious mind is the objective mind that rules the inner world. The subconscious mind is very powerful and its energy is obtained from the *Mind of God*. However, the objective mind does not engaged in the process of proving or judging, but just follow orders. The subconscious mind never rest or sleeps and is a Universal Source of power directly connected with **Universal Mind.**

Oftentimes, there are problems you face that are beyond your ability and power to transform them. However, you can entrust your problems through meditation into the silence to gain knowledge to soften your fears, worries, and transform the difficulties to victory. Whether you want to resonate with love, health, wealth or success you can always depend on **The Source** and through a fist of faith God will share *His* wisdom with you, and grant you all your wishes.

Sometimes when event happens in our lives do not meet our expectations, especially in a financial situation. When there is a short fall of money to pay your bills that have piled up. Even if you have managed to pay a small amount on these bills, it did not solve the entire problem. It seems as though you will never escape this overwhelming situation.

When you mind is full of clutter and overwhelmed this only leads to more confusions and difficulties, because your ego will add more fears and worries into this unfavorable dilemma. Unless you are awake and start meditating on your *Inner Knowing* for help during these crises to still the mind and guide the mind to resonate with the right vibrational thoughts and hear the answer from within and transport yourself from problems towards a favorable position, to release you from the conditions of debt that has imprisoned you from accumulating wealth, freedom to do the things you really desire to do.

When you understand the clarity of your emotions can influence the stream of your thoughts. You will become more vigilant and align with your *Source*, because you don't want to be trapped by the ego's anxiety again! The more familiar you are with your mind the more peaceful it becomes. When your mind is calm and peaceful, and you are free from discomfort of ego and are free to experience the true happiness.

The fastest way to resolve your problems is to surrender your situation to the invisible source of God. You can try the following statement.

Dear God, you said, "*I have done all I can, I surrender my whole heart and situation to your hands.*"

Then, you let go of all your attachments that you face and move on. Since you have truly surrendered to God, you feel the burden on your shoulders has been lifted. Gradually, you notice that your life has begun to change, because you have listened and acted upon God's guidance and more opportunities will be attracted to you and lead to increase of power to generate better income.

Your financial situation improves because of your spiritual relationships with God has tightened. You believe, you can always find fulfillment and this trust in God will change in your life.

Chapter Ten
~The Power of Peace—Patient
•Endurance•Affirmative•Calmness•Eternity~

For years, I was determined to re-build the life style I desired, and then I awaken to the world within me and it holds me in their understanding, it's timeless, in which I see every change and is full of joy and happiness. I don't lash out at myself over what I think is intended to happen to me. I don't grip onto life anymore, and started to recognize who I am and I can't lose anything. I began to learn that an invisible Divine love, with a great magnitude lives within me and is created to recognize that peaceful feeling inside, if I simply let go to learn and understand its Divine power to show me the loveliness reflected within itself.

I consciously resonate with my *Source* in an effective way to achieve a complete attunement with the *Universe*. I begin to visualize myself where I desire to be. Each energy block I add with joy and inner peace according to the vision I perceive. I then realize I truly live with my motives, thoughts, and acts to keep whatever thought dominates me and support my life, my goals towards sustaining my heart's desires.

I magnify my own vision, where I can perceive the highest potential and see myself resting in the sunshine surrounded by nature in peace and the sensations of absolute joy to join with harmony and my nature declaration of inner stillness, peacefulness, and fearlessness, which is calling from within. I know I am no longer sustaining a life that is affected by the outer world. I feel like I am losing, but indeed I am gaining something more powerful than I thought. By persisting right thinking, I repeatedly experience **The Source** energy consistently filling me with joy, peace, and contentment and feel the invitation of love by the *Divine*, where *He* is living in the center of my heart. I have experienced total transformation and physical change. I begin to understand the "I" will never change, but I am in one with this *Source* energy.

I do not cease thinking of old problems, but have the abilities to imagine endless series of solutions and to awaken to the higher understanding that allows me to transcend the need to live with every painful experience and walk through the discomfort and confine them. I do not forcefully reject thoughts entering into my conscious mind; I acknowledge their presence and let them fade. I pay attention to my thoughts, which I have, the power to direct and control their flow into my mind. I have trained my mind to obey my will. When my mind is operating along positive lines, I feel strengthened and empowered to carry out my intention and progress on my road to succeed. Even though, the *Inner Knowing* is invisible to me, but it is capable of influencing the emotional feelings in me.

They reside in my subconscious mind and rarely make themselves known in obvious ways. I become aware of their presence when I decided to make changes in my life. The best part of this is that I don't need to believe how something is possible, but simply willing to believe it is and is often already good enough to affect and to attract change.

I believe my mind is capable of painting many great pictures, because it is limitless to what can be imagined and achieved in the physical world. I intuitively know that the greatest treasure is living inside and every event regardless of its nature is coming to help deepen my understanding and further the development of my soul. I live in a peaceable state of self-realization and no place more empowering than to be in the present moment. Similarly, I know how to meet each moment and find within its meaning to evolve stronger, wiser, and more grateful of being alive.

I want my path to lead me to a peaceful place, but the path is there before me. My task is to connect with **The Source** that lives inside of me. I continue to develop the direct relationship with my *Inner Source* that I am a part of an emerging with. I have invited it into my life, live with it, and become more receptive to the signals I hear and acknowledge. Follow this way to learn, to let go and to live in the present, I know I can't fail in my wish to follow God's peace.

My thought and feelings reassure me that I am able to connect to ideas and create them. Since I am able to capture ideas from the silence of my inner thoughts and let my mind rest upon them knowing that every thought will respond to itself. The "yes, I can and I will," generates the idea to form the desire in my mind. Consciously, I use the Invisible Universal power to produce my desires, I understand all space is filled with creative power of thought and the creative power is amendable. I affirm every thought with my subconscious mind and keeping the faith on the power to overcome any adverse situation. It is word of faith that sets me free, not faith in any specific thing or act, but simply faith all things. It is faith that gave me peace within my heart and believes everything is possible for me.

When you experience the peace consciousness within, then real peaceful events will happen to you. The external environment is a physical acknowledgement within the inner spiritual awareness. It is the shift of the inner consciousness, which makes us all unique.

When you think and act accordingly to your inner guidance leads to the power of your thought drawn from within. Then not only do you allow the Light consciousness to shine through your physical being, but you also infuse this inward power into your conscious mind and connect yourself with strength and endurance, which will enable you to solve the problem effortlessly and effectively, and in confidence with faith and peace.

Your subconscious mind will scan your mind for stress and conflicts and assess your environment for danger and remove you to safety. In this way, your thoughts and feelings are more lucid and as a result it will bring forth the condition you want in life. You may find many solutions to your problem can be resolved through inner silence during meditation to focus and to take heed of the power of your subconscious to affect and change any condition in the old environment. You can achieve serenity and hope through meditation, because it helps you to focus on inner peace and improves the quality of your life significantly. You need to understand how your subconscious and conscious mind works and how they interact with each other. You will be able to transform your whole life to live peacefully. It is also important for you to know that everything is possible when you hold on to a strong belief in your subconscious power.

You don't need to be a genius to know everything; if you know how to engage your inner power, anything is possible. Picture the ideal conditions, visualize the success in your mind and imagine yourself already in the position and feel the positive energy influencing you. Do not acknowledge limitations, or do not allow any other suggestion to lodge in your mind other than success and the faith to have this fulfilled. It will prevent you from derailing from the chosen path. When you are certain of your choices, gradually you will find the shortest route.

By following the basic principles of peace consciousness, you are walking towards the light in your spiritual journey and you know it is already yours in the limitless Universal supply.

If you open your heart to your *Inner Source* you will perceive what this experience is telling you, about your attitude and your own spiritual nature? It is your inner thoughts surrendering to love and peace, which will roll away your troubles entirely. When you attune to your inner journey and learn to control your thoughts and emotions will translate your desire into love; this state of oneness is the condition to meet all your needs and will improve your life, because of this innate power to bring all your desires, fulfillments, and peace in your life.

You must understand that this change is coming from inside before it manifests into the conscious mind. So you use imagination to create what you want from the *Inner Source*. You are actually living in the world of dreams. You choose the highest view by realizing that whenever you see, hear, or think you fill with your imagination so it will expand to a broader reality and automatically bring you the substance you desire. The world you want to live in is through the power of your imagination to create, and the willingness to go beyond your physical reality. You know your real success comes from within the internal world for knowledge, wisdom, and peace. You find higher potential, because of your faith and belief in its innate power to deliver the objective reality.

Your inner ability continues to grow because of your understanding of peace and by tapping into your inner strength to envision your success and growth. Your ability to awaken to the higher self allows you to transcend the need to live abundantly. It is not sufficient to ponder this thought, but to understand your relationship with your inner self to know of the peace that lives in you. You must be able to respond, when you hear a little voice talking to you without interruption. It is your most reliable source of guidance through your journey to find peace and harmony. It is important to know that your *Higher Source* is your friendly ally and can be trusted. You have total control of the awareness in your life, because you have learned to emerge with your inner thoughts to create the condition to work peacefully and you will always know beyond reasonable doubt that if you follow these gentle suggestions you will be where you want to be. It is your peaceful intent in your subconscious that brings you eternal peace and love. You fill yourself with **The Source** of peace by opening to its influence so that you carry this with you wherever you go. Thus, you become a magnet to attract peace from all sources and to some extent you are able to use it to help others.

You become more aware of your inner serenity and you speak and act on peace without any conditions. You have developed the ability to let go of something you don't need. After you let go of your desire you come to realization that you have opened the door to the entrance of peace and harmony.

You have learned to embrace the beauty of nature and recognize it is part of the *Universal Creative Life Force*. It proves by itself that nature has barrenness and every life is sustained.

When you open yourself to embrace perfect peace, the world will embrace you. You build your strength, by conserving it. You are opening your heart and then you accept the love in you. The joyous vibrations that you share with others still remain.

You let God enter into your world more fully and let it express itself through you. You experience the coincidence of miracles emerging to you soon. Life in itself is abundant. You feel perfectly peaceful and return to the path of joy and blissfulness.

God awaken your heart to various channels and directs your mind towards the right path and now you can gain more power to enriching your spiritual life, financial success, love, and health. You are aware of your life force comes from the connection to this *Invisible Source* and by merging with **The Source** of your power, you can gain more success and abundance and also raise your consciousness. It gives you the ability to relate and communicate from the body, mind, and spirit and provides the best method to navigate through life.

It was one sunny evening two years ago, when I was sitting in a tranquil spiritual room by myself. Then, I discovered an increase of spiritual energy and suddenly there was a clearer awareness of spiritual thought that alerted me to an extraordinary event that was about to happen in my life. It said that I should continue to focus on the *Higher Self* and spend more time meditating and making conscious connection to **The Source** to achieve new experiences as directed by the *Higher Self*. I also realize at that moment the spiritual energy enveloped my whole body. I know meditation is one way of expanding inner abilities, and mind awakening. I believe this is a sign that leads my life's purpose with greater joy and doors open and various paths will be clear. Now it is up to me to choose what brings the greatest return.

I started to relax my mind, let go, eliminate tensions, which normally produce physical exhaustion and meditate through the consciousness to the power within. I let things be and allow my *Inner Self* to be free to see life flowing to me. I closed my eyes and sat quietly. In the beginning the mind usually bounces around from thought to thought. I realize I have neither control of the mind activities nor the movement of my physical body. I still hear a lot of background noises that disturb my concentration. However, after sitting for 10 minutes, the mental activity of the mind begins to relax and I experience the deep bodily relaxation bursts within me and blossomed into a peaceful sensation of greatness. It is motionless and at this point **The Source** takes over and a blissful feeling of victory takes place.

The limitation of self is transcended and is evaded. I continue concentrating on one subject and not worry about the external events. I know at this moment I may be in the most receptive stage of the process of gaining self-assurance. I focus on the subject of "peace" and slowly penetrates deeper into the silence space of "peacefulness" and then I feel complete silence within. Through the silence I realize my true nature is always there, and in all situations and circumstances and at no time it falls away.

I also chant the echo of God sounds "Ah" and focuses on its energy to get off any thought that wants to penetrate into the mind. I continue to meditate on the sound of God and use the sound as an attractor for manifesting peace in me. I know I like to attract the sense of blissfulness and peaceful sensation in me. I am chanting the resonance of God sounds vibration the "Ah" silently. I feel complete peace with an unlimited happiness, and freedom felt from within. I realize that "Ah" symbolizes the Divine word and the entire Universe is connected and this energy does bless us.

Now, I won't exchange it for anything else. I felt a complete freedom without any reservations in my state of inner consciousness of peace. I know I have succeeded to gain this power of internal peace with consciousness binding me to the power of the *Divine Light* and love.

I enter into a new phase of my life for eternal peace in my heart. I began to understand the physical world is perceived from within and projected to the external consciousness. I know I have found wisdom, knowledge and purpose and an unlimited flow of infinite supply from within.

Opportunity emerges to me effectively and easily. I attain great blessings of genuine good health. I recognize these potentialities within; therefore, it benefits me in the external world. I believe God always has a plan for everyone through an awakened relationship with "*Him*" and make conscious contact in the silence and feel "*His*" love.

Often, our concept seems to come from a remote place and shows up suddenly in a flash of light and disappears for a moment. The physical world may still have many existing problems, but there are always inner resources that we can tap into and easily overcome these problems. There are no problems so big that your *Inner Source* cannot resolve. You can always find calmness and peace within. Life is abundant, but life is never filling with lack. When you have inner peace your life is full of Divine abundance and will never burn out.

You realize it is important to give than just to receive. You can receive anything you want simply by giving to others. When you apply this rule to love, it will be the same. If you want love to emerge, and you must give love to others without holding anything back. You must feel the love in you before you can offer your love towards others. You must not keep any hidden agendas because if you do, it will destroy the whole purpose of the *Law of Giving and Receiving*. It is a joyful event that you offer help to each other so that everyone can benefit. The ultimate goal to giving is not to expect anything in return that is the genuine idea of the condition of love.

Your generous gift will bring joy and happiness to others and you. In return, it brings forth desirable conditions with unlimited flow of energy through the *Universal Creative Life Force* of unlimited supply and abundance.

The wisdom from within has given you a full awareness of the circumstances and conditions as above and so below you in the physical world to experience peace. You perceive a vision of peace from within and project this to become your physical veracity. Experiences have given you many opportunities to learn, to grow, and to build a great harmonious, interactive relationship with the *Universal Creative Life Force*.

We must connect peace with the collective consciousness souls of people around the globe and together we will bring peace to the world. We must take some action to bring harmony to this Earth and create a better place for everyone to live through the power of peace consciousness. With everyone involved, speaking out and acting on it, will extend and promote a peaceful environment to the world. This will create a peaceful vision into God's global plan to initiate world peace and love. We must be vigilant about this goal of peace and attribute a condition of God's love to someday see a new world of peace.

Your life will transform as soon as you recognize this inner energy and will give you the freedom to vision the kind of life you chose to live. This positive energy transcends from the body, mind, and spirit to produce the influence you will have in your life. It is through the subconscious mind and right thinking, that you are connected to the peaceful force and love. (*For example, every day, I am heal and getting better and better*)

Your prayer will be answered if you continue to focus on the lens of the imagination on what you seek and create. You must believe whatever you imagine can happen now and be prepared to open to new horizons discovering unique qualities appearing in your life. You must believe the power of success is through the recognition, acceptance, and alignment with the *Divine* and the results will deliver an unstoppable flow of wealth into your life. When you understand how the subconscious and conscious mind operates, you are able to attract anything you truly desire.

The subconscious power within will help you to achieve the higher capacity of financial success, personal advancement and spiritual enlightenment. By applying the power within, you are aligned with your *Source* and this energy will continue to flow with joy and love radiates into your heart.

You are living in a bountiful Universe with unbounded supply and abundance through utilizing the power of thought. As your inspiration deepens and gains momentum, you must realize for everything to be successful you must be detached from your relationships with struggle, fear, and worry.

You realize these kinds of self-imposed roadblocks are a hindrance. These obstacles are found in the low energy field and you should rapidly replace them with positive attitude towards your original intent. When you are in the stream of abundance, you know what is best for you. You will gain new life energy and a greater power each day, and you understand that everything you wish for will transform into a positive ending.

You feel happy when you know you are guide to your purpose and follow your heart. Your truth is God's peace within. Your attention is drawn to that dim-light within, which bring you purpose and desire, and is filled with harmony. Focus your energy on that *Inner Light* is the connection to your *Inner Knowing*. Merge with your *Inner Knowing* and keep your faith that the Universal Mind will provide, and acknowledge your request and will exert this with the power of intention. When you choose to trust that Inner Knowing to manifest your desire, immediately you are certain of everything you hoped for and is in natural rhythm according to your faith, believe you shall receive it soon.

Divide the word PEACE into five separate letters; you get

P	---------------------	PATIENT
E	---------------------	ENDURANCE
A	---------------------	AFFIRMATIVE
C	---------------------	CALMNESS
E	---------------------	ETERNITY

These five words are perfectly matched with the singularity of the word *peace*. When you contemplate on these words, you realize they are closely related to each other. Therefore, it is my hope that the loveliness and attentiveness of these attractive words will give you the inspirational stillness and serenity. I hope these words will bring you inner peace and tranquility, change you, and eliminate stress, fear and doubt and the intention of living with the awareness of the thought of peace.

If you want to receive any inspirational thoughts, you must be very patient so that you can lie back quietly listening to the voice echoing back to you and everything becomes abundantly clear. However, if you want your desires manifested to you and this is not happening. It is because everything has a Divine time line. When you push for a manifestation the results may not be as you wish for.

However, when you are patiently waiting everything will come to you naturally and effortlessly. You can see a better picture. Your ability to stay awake will separate failure from success. Then, **The Source** will help you to create the life of your choice. You have a clear vision and faith in the outcome to wait patiently for this success.

Furthermore, you will feel more relaxed even if it has not occurred instantly, but you continue to stay focused on making your request knowing to the *Universe*, you will feel that your demands are being deposit into your life. You continue to feel its vibration respond to you.

Endurance gives you the abilities to tolerate prolong hardships and difficulties and stay calm. When the end comes, you will see a rainbow emerge to you. You know for every effect to happen there must be a cause and is followed by an effective result. An action must occur before any event can take place. Trust that everything happened has a *Divine* purpose and believe what you feel deeply within you will be filled by your own intention and purpose. Therefore, when the end is near, it will bring you a sense of joy and happiness. View the events you consider as obstacles and is a perfect opportunity to resolve and find your peace. Difficulties and problems are no longer a stress issue and you know your problems will prevail because of the power of **The Source** in you. Success comes to you when you are aware of **The Source** power and are one with this and you have the faith, the trust and the peace inside to meet the conditions that success is build upon.

Tolerance towards every circumstance will give you an inspirational match and the inner peace to reach for the sources strength. Endurance gives you the power to forgive yourselves. It helps you to understand these painful experiences are only temporary.

Most importantly, you must believe you did not create these blunders to displease yourself. It is part of the spiritual journey to experience life before you reach triumph.

Now you fully understand the importance and the meaning of patience and endurance and now you can move on to build an affirmative belief system of inner peace.

I always encourage people to learn and live in the Now. It is the now where you continue to evolve and live with your dream. It is **The Source** energy giving you the power of success and peace.

Your affirmative attitude of knowing who you really are and accept that you can't change what God has created in you. You affirm you are more than merely a physical body and have an infinite soul will make it easier for you to acknowledge your *Inner Source* within you. You then understand it is **The Source** dwelling within your body, but not your body living within the spirit. Now you know the truth and it is fully present and available at all times. Sometime, it is difficult to accept **The Source** as dwelling within you. It is a normal response to reject or descent from this truth.

Looking at it might seem crooked or silly, but indeed it has a deeper purpose that is concealed and is waiting to be decoded.

Until you fully understand what is in store for you and what seems to be imperfect indeed, it is absolutely perfect by itself.

It is your best interest to submit all undesirable problems to **The Source**. You know and trust your *Source* will accept any unwanted dilemma from you. Afterward, be thankful for the wonderful gift of being able to break the iceberg and obstacles. See all the successes, and pains with a gratitude. You are here for a purpose and this is the key to feeling fulfilled.

When you feel calm and peaceful, you are dwelling in love and with peace. Your thoughts are lucid and supple and without fear and worry, and live life to serve others. You penetrate into a moment of complete serenity and seemingly everything is motionless, no noise but silence. Therefore, you feel completely peaceful.

You do not judge on how others will judge you, but remain true to yourself and the peace that abides in you. Your mind is empty and thoughtless. As soon as, you quiet your mind you will feel you are able to take on the world and any situation put in front of you. You believe this power of peace brings you infinite love, joy, and compassion. You feel the endless peace and the omnipresence and omnipotence of the power of God. You call "*Him*" great. Now you are aware of "*His*" greatness and "*He*" is truly great.

You are in touch with this greatness. The greatness is the whole *Universe* behind you. You leave your desires, ambitions, and concerns behind. You see things as they are without trying to dominate and control them. You accept yourself and the world accepts you. Everything begins with peace and the assurance of the eternal peace and the highest energy to reach fulfillment.

Chapter Eleven
~Tolerance—Open-Mindedness~

Tolerance is the acceptance of differing views of other people without being bias or prejudice. When your mind is attentive the amount of tolerance towards the hostility of others will be higher. If a person is open-minded, he is able to assess a complex situation that is set in front of him. Intolerance is the unwillingness to accept other people's viewpoint that is different from you, or attempting to apply force towards others to agree with you and accept your opinions on your terms. Person, who is center with his thoughts of inner-peace, can tolerate any unpleasant events and remain calm and his body is unresponsive to pain. His inner-mind is separate from all external tortures, but continues perceiving peace and joy in communicating to God. He believes the peace of God will take care of everything. For this to happen a person mind needs to discover a way of detaching his *Inner-self* from the outer environment. In other words, a person brain needs to successfully trigger an escape route to separate from his tormentors and psychologically replaced them with ecstasy and a clear mind. Consequently, he no longer feels pain as part of his discomfort and is capable of expanding beyond the limits of the body from mental pain to peace, calmness, silence, and consolation.

There is an old saying do not judge a book by its cover. In other words, do not judge a person merely by looking at him without knowing him, his history or background or personality before making any judgment. However, I came across this statement from a source five years ago and found it fascinating, "**beware do not be fooled by a person charming appearance or personality.**"

When events happen, it is possible to take two different forms of handling the situation. One can ignore the circumstances as nothing is happening or attempting to interfere with the dilemma. Your intuitive urging warns you to be aware of dealing with strangers. You are advised to listen to your instinctive power, they are precise and very deliberate and most importantly, they will never blunder. I remember meeting this person ten years ago by chance. During this meeting I sensed a tremendous amount of negative vibrations released from him. As soon as he left the room a quiet voice whispers to me, "hey, take caution while dealing with him." I hesitated! I know I am always capable of tolerating people's behavior or attitude. In other words, I do not form discriminative opinions or defy others, unless I have a strong indication that negativity surrounds those people. It was an inner feeling of intolerance that suddenly occurred and deep inside my inner-calmness there was confusion and discomfort that had influenced my judgment towards that person. In fact, the forewarning and precaution was absolutely right, but I found out he was a con artist. He had scammed from many people in his inner circle before he expired from the planet Earth. I felt bestowed, because I listened to my inner voice and defied that person.

When you open your heart to others, you accept who they are without favoritism or reservation. You help them wholeheartedly without any hesitation. You do not reserve any doubt or raise questions about their creditability, because you treat them equally and fairly. You open your heart to God, so that others can come to you for help or advice. People may not fully understand you, but you continue offering them love and help, and treat them like a real friend. You have adopted the quality of compassion, benevolence, loving and caring personality and are like God's omnipresent of peace and the joy you extend to them. You know this is your inborn nature. You enjoy giving love and caring for others without expecting anything in return. You guide them through difficulties without holding back. You love all people and the Universal peace. This is a true nature of a humanitarian.

Chapter Twelve
~Synchronicity~

The coincidences of events seem related, but it may not be consciously know by you or others. Synchronicities are people, places, or events that your soul attracts into your life—to help you evolve to a place that emphasize your position in life. Not all synchronically events are desirable. Sometimes, it is just a coincidence and for you to learn new experiences, so you must be very conscious of its substance. Often, if you are unaware, your weaken mind could attract negative entity, which will cause a drama to unfold which may bring harm to you or may cause a short or long term affects.

When you meet someone through the introduction of a special event, immediately, you feel a bond with this person and are connected. In this case the karma between this person and you is positive, but in some other cases you attract other people for the purpose of advancement and definitely you shall receive help from them, because of your involvement during that social event.

In the fast track world, we have met many people who have entered into our lives. Some of them emerge for a longer period of time, but a number of them are here for only a short time. However, these people are connected to you and their relevance does have an effect on you.

Strangely enough you don't need to know them to be connected. These are driving forces in the *Universe* that will subconsciously connect you to them either directly or indirectly.

Occasionally, we might connect to people in a very weird or unexpected way. But, you must pay special attention to those connections. Undesired event could occur due to your inattentiveness or lower energy causing listlessness in your physical body. This scenario leaves your mind at sleep drifting back and forth into a different dimension and feeling that you are on an airplane, unknown and unexpected to you. You had no idea where you are at that moment, but connected to this external event without being aware. By default, you have accepted everything that comes forth to you, because you were unconscious. Your sleepiness was impartial and far from ordinary. It has clouded your senses and turned your world into a dream. However, you can escape this unwanted scenario by consciously awake to the *Now*. As soon as you are awakened in the *Now*, then the undesirable scenario will vanish and the presences of growing stronger, by centering your mind you have enabled yourself awake to your conscious awareness of what is around you.

Other synchronically event occurs when one or two replicated events happen in your life and you are mindful about them. These two significant events have brought you tremendous luck. These kinds of auspicious moments might or might not be a coincidental, but your higher self is connected to them. It is the invisible Universal power, which creates this great event.

It could happen one day and you are invited to a spiritual exhibition, and a sudden urge guides you to walk towards one of the booths and you discovered the information that you have been looking for some time and finally it emerges to you with great surprise. This explains the events, which happen are in tune with the *Universal Mind* and your thoughts and happened as they should. Nothing can happen without a reason. It is possible at that moment your instincts are driving you towards your desires.

For every event to happen it needs a cause and effect, and is directed by a creator, who determines how far he will go and what the result will be. It is all forming in your mind as to how you want to accomplish it.

You are eagerly waiting to receive an item, but it has not arrived yet. Unknown to you the event has already manifested in a different dimensional place, but is not present to you. This has taken place for a reason, but the item was misdirected to your neighbor's mail box. You are about to call the post office to enquire about it, before you picked up the phone and dialed, then a neighbor knocked at your door and "this must be for you my friend" he said. The item did arrive, but was in the wrong place; however there is order and synchronicity with the connection to all events.

I believe, you notice there are certain numbers have special affect on your life and follow you wherever go. A personal number that I am attached is seven (7).

This number is very significant to me and I am connected with this for a number of years and I am still conscious of its presence. For example, my house number, email address, phone numbers are connected with the number seven. Its spiritual power cannot be escaped.

There are certain events we could avoid if we listen to our *"Higher Self."*

For example, a man was warned by a psychic twenty years ago about a person whom he met whose surname began with a *"M"* could possibly bring harm to him. He must be very leery of this person, if by chance he meets him. Unfortunately, he ignored and defied this particular warning. As a result, the damages were immeasurable.

Therefore, we must listen to messages delivered to us, because it will save us from unhappy incidents. God has sent you a message through a messenger, but you must not defy it. A twist of fate likes this is too valuable to be ignored.

Due to a landslide, a man was ordered to move out of his house. Twenty minutes was given to him to remove everything from his house. However, the insurance does not cover unnatural causes. It looked as if he lost everything. He removed the painting out of his house and found out later that it was worth 50 million dollars more than his original price of $20. Now he could rebuild his house.

Your faith and belief that you have everything needed from the *Universe* and the *Universe* will provide you with more and there is no lack. You must take action to receive what you desire, but the action must be inspired by spirit, then it will emerge to you effectively and effortlessly.

Chapter Thirteen
~The Power of Giving Money~

If you desire more money to come your way, maybe you should consider giving money away to achieve this objective. The *Universal Law of Giving and Receiving* states that the more you give away and more money will show up at your door, but you must do it with a clear mind. The best ways to give money is giving with no hidden agenda in the mental mind, but follow your heart urges and give truly. The *Universe* will respond to your heart, but not to how much money you have given away. Your money is just a token symbol and has no real meaning to the Universe. Your motivation to give money generously without conditions will bring an inner joy and happiness to you. When you contribute a gift to community, you feel you belong there. You wish to show you're caring. You are enthusiastic about your involvement and the enthusiasm to change and improve people's lives. You believe it gives you an opportunity to spark that inner benevolence to share with others. You feel the fortune you accumulated over the years and this is the time to donate some of that back that would benefit others. This idea comes to you, because God's love has triggered your inner passion and reminds you to share your wealth with people. Now, you progressively believe giving funds to help the neediness has brought a greater joy and peace in your infinite self. It also shows that you are grateful to the *Universe* and allow the Universal flow of life to continue to enlarge on the richness of life that will benefit others more.

You understand that the infinite energy in the *Universe* is connected to you and others therefore when you offer a gift to help others it will always benefit the life of the people around you and you know this kind of energy will always return to you to be multiplied, because it allows the flow to continue to grow and expand.

You know giving money will continue enriching your soul and sustain life. It continues to replenish the Universal flow of unlimited supply and abundance touches many people hearts and as it does for everyone who activates the act of giving.

You want to accumulate wealth to you then you need to give money away to show your benevolence and love and the appreciation of your kindness. Give it to friend who helps you to stay in touch with the inner world. Give it to people, who help you, heal you, love you, and inspire you. Give it to people without expecting them to return it, because this is the real treasure held in your heart and this has value and will always continue to increase.

Today it is fashionable for businesses to detonate their money to charity and this benevolence is share to help others in the community. This giving leads to accumulating more wealth, because of your generous heart in helping others. Don't be too stingy with money. Money comes from abundance, but not scarcity. Give without expectation, but *do* expect return.

As you do you will see your own wealth grow. You have believed in your spiritual self, in abundance, in love and when the Universe hears your intention of giving to the world. It does not come as a reward, because you genuinely believe abundance and love exist.

Imagine a scenario you have never donated money before, because you do not feel you can. You are thinking of lack of funds in your bank account therefore, you are hesitated and reluctant. A recent report shows that people, who gave money, have received a sum of money back from unknown sources for their heartfelt support. You give money because you feel good to do so.

I remembered I made a vow few years ago, on every of my birthday I will donate funds to Vancouver Children Hospital Funds. I feel it serves me right and is a right cause and I feel the spiritual nourishment and in which it gives me a sense of joy and peaceful connection with the *Universe* and has the effect of opening prosperity to flow. The *Universe* is a huge place where wealth can come from many different resources, not just come from any avenue. To give is always in my heart and I desire to do so. It reminds me because of self, peace, and love. I also believe true giving is done anonymously.

You give money and it is from your heart, but the *Universe* knows what you do and will return something back and when it does, it will surprise you and lift your spirits. The joy of giving is a reflection from within and the moment of happiness that you always will remember.

Giving money is not a competition and you must give without any condition or string attached. You simply give generously from your heart to deepen your soul.

Do not belittle others when you give, let others see a vision of your generous heart. It is a bad idea to think of others needing to beg you for money. Let others see the world with a different view. It gives people a chance to see sharing is in everyone's heart. Everyone can benefit from God's unlimited supply of Universal abundance and wealth. There is plenty in this huge pie to share with one another and it is in exhaustible commodity.

Give money from your heart. *Feel the blissfulness*

In fact, you definitely feel blessed, because the invisible *Universe* has given you a chance to serve, and the appreciation of your own skills, and the abilities to achieve long-term success. You understand what your financial contribution can do to benefit others, enrich, and improve their lives. Therefore, it is an honor to give truly and it will be reduced or eliminated lack, but increase happiness and promotes the quality of living to benefit each other. You will receive a response from the Universe to acknowledge your good deeds. You will be surprised to discover how quickly the *Universe* response to your act of giving to others. Giving is a reflection of your inner self to the external consciousness.

Your motivation to give money is because you are showing your gratitude to the *Universe* for the unlimited supply and you wish to keep the *Universe* flow of life continuing to manifest endlessly. We all have so much to give, and surely if everyone did it, we would change the world.

Giving and receiving will activate the eternal flow of life. When someone offers you a gift accept it gratefully. However, you are also free to reject this gift, but it will not block any future abundance coming to you.

Money must be allowed to flow without restrain, so that it will benefit many and keep the energy continuing to flow forever and return freely. You know you have activated the *Universal Law of Giving and Receiving* when you have acknowledged your heart intention and do benefit everyone.

I have been discussing about giving let me explain how it works. It's your generous feelings to give and you are in the flow of yourself. You have been blessed in your life and the *Universe* knows what you deserve. We must give without expectation of return and the Universe will take care of the rest.

Giving might not necessarily involve money. It can be information that you sent to your friend and this information can lead to a resolution of a problem.

It was ten years ago a friend of mind asked this person if he could connect him to a company so that he could submit a proposal to them. He replied "I will help you, what will I get in return." My friend thought about his answer and responded to him, "I will get back to you." This person had blocked the energy of the *Universal Law of Giving and Receiving* to flow through him, because he does not recognize the power of selflessness and being able to help others, and then the *Universe* will take care of the reciprocal part.

If people can truly dedicate themselves to give real service to help others this will make a big difference in the lives and others. If you want to gain success in your life you must apply the *Universal Law of Reciprocal* and will attract to you more than you can expect. The *Universe* knows what you give, but someday many good things will return to you because it is natural *Laws of Abundance*.

One thing you need to understand about this law, it is not about what you expect to receive, but acknowledge the real principal of giving and receiving. It is the basic principal of what you sow so shall you reap. The importance is you give a gift to help others with joys in your heart and without conditions or expectation of a return. You donate funds because you are inspired by the inner consciousness and motivate you to give money and to carry on with your innate ability to create the condition of living for others, a developing service to help someone become independent and successful. Your motivation and intention is understandable, because it serves the purpose of giving and receiving.

The pure intention of giving is making good use of your skills and enabling others to reach for their goals of a better life. The energy of your thought vibrations soon attracts more abundance to you. Consequently, you receive a reward from the Universe, because *The Source* is impartial to everyone. Hence, it meets with the requirement of what you sow so shall you reap. The good things continue to flow forever in the *Universe* and returns to you.

Some people did not give because they feel lack or can't afford to give. It is a flaw in their thought patterns and the fear of scarcity. As soon as you think of scarcity the energy of lack attracts less to you. You should not let fear affect your ability to give money away. Fear in your mind will attract more unwillingness to giving. You also do not think abundantly, and are unable to visualize a beneficial image of giving in your mind. When you give fearlessly many amazing surprises will return to you someday. Your belief creates the experience of the power of giving and every time it comes it is a wonderful feeling of passing on the gift.

Every time you feel grateful it is because you have given back to community and helping others. You are glad to share your gratitude with others. In that moment, you feel a sense of greatness and never felt the shortage again. You realize that every time you have given money it has brought you more abundance into your life. You have activated the *Universal Law of Abundance* continuing to flow your way. The *Universe* knows you deserve to receive what is flowing back to you.

I feel joyful and grateful for what I can do to help others. I always like to share with others. When I was living in Cornwall in England, I started sharing great things with many new friends I met and know that I was following my bliss and was led by my inner consciousness. Thirty years today I still do it, because I continue feeling the great joy and happiness in my heart.

Wait for the right moment to give and this will add more joys and happiness to your action of giving. I tell you why I say that. I saw an advertisement on TV a couple nights ago regarding donating coins for kids. As soon as I saw this adv I knew I was going to do something. These coins I have collected over the years are in the treasure box sitting on top of the fireplace unattended. And now I am glad I can do something with them. While I was writing this chapter of giving money suddenly, the adv revisit my consciousness and reminds me to take these coins to Save-on-Food Coins Collection Center so that I could help those who would benefit by my deposit. I was feeling great because I took this action.

Giving brings happiness into your life and you have activated the *Law of Reciprocity* and let the Universal abundance to flow forever and return to benefits everyone. Gift has no reservation, conditions or expectations. Let it grow, harmonizes and multiplies on its own and continue to expand infinitely. We don't know how long it will flow through the *Universe* before it returns to benefit many hearts. It is a beautiful long lasting thing and blesses many hearts across the globe and by letting the *Law of Reciprocity* to flow in the life and this will increase more benefits, when it does return.

Our attitudes, motives and Inner passion, with which we give money back to the *Universe* is the most precious gift. Our motivation to give money back to the *Universe* is because money is a way of showing our love, gratitude, and appreciation for the gifts in our life.

Give freely, regularly and generously without any expectation of return and with a joyous and blissful heart.

Chapter Fourteen
~The Power Behind Your Success~

Every one's version of success is different from one another. However, the accurate meaning of success is when you utilize the power of the inner source, in trusting and having the belief to overcome obstacles and your hindrance to success, especially adversity or difficulties and your triumph over life's setbacks is done through the power of your belief system.

You are a mogul, because of your insight, beliefs, the trust in yourself and the confidence you have in creating many business ventures and gain financial richness around the globe. You have also the opportunities to help others to succeed in their chosen fields and for them gain financial abundance. You enjoy accumulating acquisitions over the years and currently. You have the brilliance for business and the attribute for success. (For example, Donald Trump is a business genius.) It is as if you simply snap your fingers, and then things will transform and emerge to you at your desk. It sounds like magic, but is real, perfect, powerful, and amazing, because what you have built, accomplished, accumulated, and over the years has fulfilled your business ventures and guarantee of success.

Success brings a lot of satisfaction to us. Financial independence is one of the most desirable goals to achieve. Consider this; can success and money be separated from each other? It is for you to decide.

Simply put, if you want to become a lawyer you need to accumulate funds to pay for your tuition fees. You must be able to support yourself until a degree is completed. After four years of hard work you have completed the law degree and your future is incredible abundance.

Success has a price to pay. Understand it takes a lot of strength and energy and mental power to complete and obtain your degree. You believe it is worth the time and the effort and glad you took the action to complete your courses. That is one step closer to your greater successes.

Can a person gain successes without a degree. I think so!

In fact, we have the powers and abilities to succeed and this incredible power is in the power of the subliminal mind. It is through the energy of your subliminal thoughts and a strong conviction and commitment to succeed and the success is yours in the making. In the beginning you may find it perplexed and difficult, but the ultimate decision and choice is yours. You need to meet with the prerequisite and endure barriers and setbacks, but at the end of the dark tunnel there is always a silver lying. You see an arch of light of many colors; you are standing on the apex of the pyramid of achieving greater success and triumph over all difficulties and complexities.

When you determine to do something that is critical to you it is your decision and nobody can make that determination for you. However, you may hear opinions that are not so encouraging for your development. It's fine! Do not let this unsupported view discourage you. Yet, it is your project and you don't need their approval for your actions. Understand a genuine suggestions and opinions can't harm you, but there are many jealous people whose unenthusiastic vibrations can be a barrier to your success. You must avoid talking about any premature projects. Indeed, you don't need to mention nothing until your work is done. This is to protect you and your project from the *evil eye*. You need to be led by your instincts and your spiritual heart will find blissful and peace within. You never let your spirit wonder and be unattended.

If you want to succeed in your desire you must let go of control and it will emerge to you. Attachment is one of your road blocks. You need to let go of projected plans and concepts so that it will flow to you effortlessly. This is because when you charge your plan with higher expectations the negative results will turn out. Therefore, after you have done all your ground work, then sit back and relax and let nature take its course. You may be aware your work is now beyond your control and expectation, but you must remain content. Understand only contentment will bring all successes for you to thrive.

When you make mistakes in your venture, acknowledge them, and fix the problems immediately. Consider those who point out the mistakes to you are your mentors and interested in your success. You appreciate them for their insights to help you catch these blunders, so that you will not commit that fault again! It enhances and uplifts the future success of your business enterprise to reach a higher height. When you make mistakes in your endeavor recognize them, forgive yourself, and re-do again! Forgiveness will allow you to reconstruct and restore your self-confidence, self-esteem, and refine that bad experience and to do better. The healing of your experiences will help you to learn, progress, and let go of control and ultimately allow for new thoughts and ideas manifest to you. Although you must understand these principals to work for you in eliminating mistakes and poor decision and this will improve your chance of success and your venture will thrive because of your dedication.

It is essential to retain positive thoughts in the mind and charging them with positive vibrational energy. Your vigilant mind is aware of any negative thoughts or emotions, which may emerge and neutralize them with your subconscious power and the mental formation will be weakened. When your spiritual thoughts grow stronger, you are ready to transcend them into the *Universal Mind*. Your undivided thoughts and emotions resonating in the right place and continue to stay in the higher energy thought field. Positive emotions indicate you are on the right path and are a clear sign, that your goals and desires are gaining momentum in the material world.

You stay in the awareness and listen to the silence within and feel the bliss and tranquility. At present your mind is without fore thoughts. The motionless mind contains no other thought forms or interruption of mislead thoughts, but containing only the original thought and to stay in the present. When this creative thought is held long enough, then anything you wish to manifest have the potential to transmute and becomes your own reality.

Therefore, if you desire to manifest money to yourself from the *Universal Source*, have faith and believe that you have the innate power to create this moment and your wish will be granted. However, you must understand money is internal and it comes from the spirit. So, for you to receive the spirit of money you must ask the *Universe* to manifest more of these energies to you. As soon as you submit this request you must stay focus on the abundance for you to manifest this. At this point, you must filter your thoughts and act towards the significant results you want to achieve. You must pay attention to a specific thought in your mind until the objective is achieved. You will ultimately realize by staying focus in the higher energy fields of optimism, serenity, and bliss, you radiate these energies to your *Higher Self*, and the abundance will flow freely to you without resistant. Your positive feelings and emotions will indicate you are attracting a positive energy needed for the fulfillment of your heart's desire.

Finally, with everything in harmony you continue to show that you are in alignment with The Source and without missing anything. At this point, you are ready to receive what is manifesting into your life experiences from the *Universal Source* of the *Mind of God*.

The success of your venture starts from a tiny sprout and then expands this non-resistance power to attract more abundance into your life. You have thoughts of helping those who have helped you to build this successful journey. Giving thanks to others for aiding in your success will manifest more abundance into your world. Realize that people power is valuable and are the foundations of every venture in accumulating success. The personal expressions of gratitude are what sustain your belief in your purposes is, because of your strong connection to others and your willingness to extend yourself to others, and people will appreciate you and want the opportunity to work with you. Therefore, when you are rewarded for those who have helped you to succeed and you have allowed your desire to flow freely and connect to them. Opening your heart to people with passion, caring and love and faith, they will be happier to continue serving, trusting and sustaining you. As a result, you have built and attracted more solid opportunities and an unstoppable asset of capital flow into your life in the best of ways. You continue to follow your bliss, and feel like *"you are the water in the ocean, sustaining and benefiting all."*

You should pay attention to your *Inner Knowing* and be mindful before you decide on an important project or making life transformation. When you are in a hurry to make any decision or acting swiftly on something without considering your thoughts, then mistakes are made easily. But, if you are listening to that *Inner Light* and have faith in **The Source**, then there are no risks. Faith from within is connected to the center of your being and is where your purpose resides. Your purpose is to find your selflessness and your true state of being. It's a place within you from which your thoughts emerge.

It is quite possible that when you are unconsciously connected to lower energy, you weaken your ability to make mindful decision. Consequently, you have missed many significant details and busted what is almost here. However, you can change your awareness from the subjective to the objective so that you can see beyond all details and extend the abilities beyond your own boundaries; you will feel connected to your *Source*. You know that you are doing the right thing and are capable of thinking and perceiving what you want to create to the end.

When the end comes you are aware of the outcome, because you have predicted the result. You have everything within your manifested scheme to see both the horizontal and vertical. Consequently, you voice with gratitude the results of your positive action to see the end materialize and everything you needed, and the thankfulness to **The Source** for continuing to work with your steadfast purpose.

Success is not limited, but can be extended to many different professions to have their desires fulfilled. Aiming for what you desire is one of the most meaningful actions that you can take for yourself and out of the average to become the most successful, powerful and respectful person on the planet Earth. Desire will emerge to you naturally and the magnetic force can't be resisted, because it did not come directly from you. It comes from the invisible *Universe* that guides you step-by-step, structure-by-structure and synchronically follows an invisible guideline through the subconscious mind of your inner-thoughts energy and brings you the desire into your life. It is your beigness you simply return to.

You desire to share your compassion and love with people will enlarge your territory to succeed. Harmony will lead you in the best of ways. Even though the way is still formless, it will transform into form with value. The silence will show you the way, but you must continue aligning with this *Inner Light* to achieve your intention. Your path is clear and the purpose transforms from formless to form and has quality. It is you that fills this with good value to serve the world. The world becomes your refuge.

Be meek towards everything you do and to others. Throughout your life there will be changes and shifts occurring during your growth. In fact, change can occur from moment to moment to help you in the shift and make the right decision. You should always avoid any unnecessary argument and conflict with others.

Let people see your aptitude that is naturally expressed through your heart. Give blessings to the world and it will echo back to you. Your goodness will flow forever and returns to you. The other way of saying this is what comes around goes around.

Nothing in this world is perfect. Believe everything is perfect and you are deceiving yourself. Perfection there is no work to be done. There is no formula for perfection. The world is a place to learn about the relationships we have with others. You accept each other differences and abandon no one and the world is receptive to us. The wood that you carved is transformed into work of art, but still far from perfect. There are always contenders who will challenge your work, but you simply accept the root of your nature and return to harmony.

Success in spirituality could be define as a fulfillment of your personal potential, through awakening your heart and recognize the innate power within and knowing you have the abilities to fulfill every dream you have, because you are an infinite being, the unlimited potential for all that is and always will be.

Success is you recognize change is necessary in order to understand the essence of your nature so that more abundance will flow to you. Everything you created is benefiting others, because you are selfless, and are guided by spirit. You have infused everything with love.

In your heart, you know only love can help to change you or improve other's destinies. You also understand the window of opportunities will open to you through the union with your *Source*, and then **The Source** will aid you to create the life of your choice.

However, there are many factors influencing you to live a joyful and happy life. Perhaps you are experiencing temporary environmental and geographical changes in your life right now, you feel these changes have confused and prevented you from entering the higher energy field. Do not get discouraged by these mixed thoughts. You have the ability and power to override these confusions and substitute them with positive vibrations.

During the day as soon as you feel any vulnerable thoughts, just about to emerge say to yourself this—*"I have God's peace in me. I intend to carry with me wherever I go. I do not intend to change at least for now. Ah."* As soon as you say this aloud, I believe immediately you will experience a shift in your energy and soften the transformation. You will attract into your experience what you desire.

Another reason why you have experienced these blends of thoughts is because you have allowed many thoughts and ideas to penetrate into your mind at the same time and don't know which one to choose. These perplexities have confused you in many ways. Then, you stop to chew on many of them at the same time. You must separate and cancel them as soon as they emerge. Silence the mind so that you can redirect negative to positive thoughts.

From that moment you are detaching from those negative thoughts, you are able to perceive the possibility of reality. You know the moment the mind is still, and the pressure become weaken and will bring tranquility to you. Through consciousness you are drawing attention inward and listening to your heart. Gradually, you will awaken to ah, ah! You know the answers. You continue to experience and connect to the possibility of positive thought in your own reality. Now, you know you should focus your attention to vibrating a signal for activating the thought of bringing peace into your life. Only when you are learning and practicing inner-peace will you manifest the state of opportunities and receptivity and the accessibility of this peaceful state.

Nature has no desire, but only in your conscious mind. When the mind is absent of tension, fear there is just serenity and an open mind. It is complicated thoughts and ideas that manipulate the mind and you are not in the state of truly being "*you*" in your own being. However, you are always there, but your personality is not you, only in the "*Present*" you can live truly. These mixed thoughts will continue because the complex human mind is still created this way. Understand our desires are unlimited and always wanting. Unless desire stops, then you will penetrate into the moment of inner peace and silence. This is the moment you are waiting for the "inner peace and silence" is here and present, just "be" and you are fully in the present, or it is the *Present* you are truly yourself.

Everyone is hoping to make more money to carry out their plans and release their concerns and worries. However, it is not money that causes us the feeling of restlessness, but it is due to the thoughts of scarcity at that moment of not being there. It is because you want more money and refuses to reconcile for less in your current situation. Consequently, you have attempted to narrow that gap because of lack of vigilance you are not successful. You have not truly listened to the dim Light within. More conflicts are created in the mind and due to lack of insight, you are not present, and not feeling grateful for what you have, but still waiting and wanting more.

You will not see, or hear. You are totally absent from consciousness. To receive more abundance from The Source, your total presence is required.

You continue to demand extra from the external world, but receive many unrealistic thoughts to return to you. You must be aware of where to ask to fill your wishes. For everything to exist in the physical world we must "be" before we can "do" and, we must do before we can "have" and has God's omnipresence and some degree of consciousness. Through the power within you can ask for more abundance and influence in your life.

There are no rights or wrong on how much money is needed to resolve our wants. It is all in the calculation of your mind. However, there is only one deal you can settle for is peace. When you are dwelling in peace you will begin to see inner joy and happiness and the gap of wanting become less and diminished into the dim light. You begin to see how nature works miraculously in your favor. Suddenly, everything emerges to you at the right time in the right place without effort. You feel the whole world is at peace and sustain you. Harmony is naturally achieved without attainting it. Ultimately, you realize richness is obtained within, but not from the material world. The real lack you have is peace in your mind. Now you know where to find the real peace and continue to feel the abundance and wealth within.

The oceanic life accepts everything with harmony and impartially. Everything connects with the deep recesses of the ocean body are welcome. It is true that diving into the depths and the feelings of calmness and peacefulness of the body and of the mind is similar to the ocean.

All organisms are living in harmony with each other. The deep sea is one of the most peaceful and beautiful places on Earth. Nature's world is very kind and treats all things equally. However, men are not treating each other fairly. Yet, if you want to succeed, you must consider helping others to fulfill their dreams. Consequently, you will have your dreams transmuted into actuality. The natural law of what comes around goes around is fair and equal to everyone.

A proper action must precede any other action for you to have your intention carried out. You projected a selfless energy and transcended it into the invisible Universe with an intention to help dreamers to fulfill their dreams. The dream flows through the Universe and subsequently gets connected to collective consciousness souls of many people with the same idea and thought, and join together become one powerful force. This good deed continues to flow across the globe. Finally, your vision to benefit others has taken form and returns to the physical world, and transmuted into actual reality with infinite flow of peace and love infused.

Harmony is the best way to embrace and see nature. Nature always gives spontaneous response and treats all organisms impartially. If you want success in your life, you need to be mindful of everything present to you. You should accept every new concept and don't be afraid to try or test them. A successful person is always keeps his mind open to assist others and rejects no one. In his heart they are all equal and treat them without prejudice and favoritism.

In his body, mind and soul he practices compassion, kindness, believes in its nature, and is always there to serve him and others. He believes in the reciprocal nature of life and knows that these things will return to him again. He believes sharing his love is the only way for him to reach the Promised Land. One man succeeds, but other man may fail because one sees promise and the other sees only lack. If you understand the truth of this statement, you will thrive in the whole world.

Contentment comes with no price and there is no price attached for contentment. It is moment-by-moment and can be stopped by you. It connects your emotional feelings of how you feel now. It is the joyous and blissful feelings that you have attained from within, which reflect to the external consciousness. It helps you to be aware of the environment surrounding you and the joy and blissful feelings that you intended are still an extension of you. You know you are an infinite being and begin to appreciate every other living organism and their extensions, and activities happening in this world. You continue to feel the silence that you enjoy and have your questions answered from the *Invisible Force*. You are awakened to what your life journey is about. Your contentment will bring the success out of you to the heights you did not expect. You recognize your consciousness and you know where to attain your success. Lastly, when you are contented, you have wealth.

When you desire to attain something and yet take no action. Because, rushing disrupts you're thought resulting in not obtaining your goals. You get upset and distress.

While you let go of control and action will allow you to attain. Then, you feel free to accept or decline. Empting your mind and you are in harmony.

Conversely, if an action is supported, a profound energy will come from your *Inner Source* into your conscious mind to urge you to take the right action. You will attract the virtue of your thoughts, which connect with the abundance of resources and helps you link to steadfastness of the problem. All these resources are leading to a solution to the problem without postponement. Ultimately, you're feeling good and in harmony with your great awareness.

Knowing others well will prevent you from falling into a manhole and strengthened your intelligence. There are sixteen types of personalities in this world. Some are passive, active, aggressive, and con artist etc. The con artist is the one you need to take extreme precaution, because they are hazards to your health and well-being. Con artist looks for ways to scam and manipulate your strengths and weaknesses to make you feel helpless. They will play on your sympathies, install in you a sense of security in trust with them, and distract you from what is really going on using lies and the mask of truth to make talk believable. However, you must use your intelligence and do not to fall into their traps and be aware con artists have no conscience and your consciousness of their presents is needed.

The invisible source of the *Universe* is impartial to every living organism and therefore is trustworthy. There are many personality types on this Earth and the chance of meeting with different personality is possible. Dissemble types are those who hide under a false appearance.

They talk very well and promise you everything, but are committed to nothing. Those types of personalities are manipulating and deceitful and are waste of time to entrust them.

It is best to defy and disbelieve them. Do not let them manipulate, and think they can control or fool you. The best ways to unravel this type of situation is to take no action and defy them. Step out of the way and let the event speaks for itself. Now relax don't worry and believe this situation is resolving itself beautifully for everyone involved.

You don't need to go to the world to know everything; you can open your heart to the world. Then, the door will open to you. If you view yourself as self-important person, you separate yourself from the world. You always thinking you are in the top of the pinnacle and others needs your help, and can't live without you. Your false thought belief is a price and must be paid in exchange for the importance of being a stand out in front of others. Then, you can gain all the attention you want from peers and rivals. In fact, you are just self proclaiming your importance and hiding your real self from your strength. You are losing your uniqueness to the ego. Your mood starts wavering, and becomes very unsteady.

Yet your temper varies moment-to-moment and until the moment of your mood become steady and returns you to normal.

A successful person views himself as being unimportance. He connects to the world with compassion that gives him greater strength and courage. He does not need others attention to have influence. He builds his confidence on his beliefs and intuition. He does not control what others do. He surrenders the control to the world. His success is built on to win the cooperation, but not to conquer others. He believes compassion will build harmony and surrounds him with love, peace and endure with nature.

After a disagreement is reconciled there should not be any resentment in the party. It is not reconciled, if you hold on to the annoyance towards the other parties. The truthful reconciliation between the parties is harmony. In the deep there are many living organisms that can live together in silence agreement. They communicate with each other in silence and live harmoniously in the deep sea.

Chapter Fifteen
~The Law of Allowing~

You contemplate what you wish for and receive what you are thinking about. Through the power of your vibrational thoughts and the blending of the *Law of Magnetic Energy* attracts whatever you desire into your life.

You have applied the Universal Laws to manifest your dreams and desires into veracity. But, before you can complete the full performance of manifesting your dream, you must allow and agree with what is occurring to you.

You use the Universe Laws to attract acquisitions in your life; however you must let the *Law of Allowing* to complete the whole process of attraction. Then, your vibrational thought begins to circle into the *Universe* and attracting the acquisitions into your life. You are telling the *Universe* what you desire to receive and emerge to you. Your emotions and feelings activate the vibrations into your thought. You consciously contemplate on it. Eventually, your thought will mix together becoming the power of one. At this point, other factors are not required to be considered in the achieving of your desire. Only the vibrational energy between your desire and you is relevant. At this moment, you need to complete the circle of the Universal flow by allowing the results to transpire to you. You intend to create your own reality and must allow it to come without restriction. Hence, you are receiving what you want in your heart's desire.

You begin to manifest your dream successfully, because you know how to apply the *Universal Laws* in precisely the way it was created.

Further, you have connected your thought words with the emotions and feelings and vibrate them with the power of your thinking mind.

It is, as if you tuned into a radio station and recognize the music you want to listen to and enjoy it. You acknowledge to the *Universe* that you are part of it. You have let the *Universe* know that you are the one who manifested this desire. You have claimed and let the *Law of Allowing* to obtain and receive this without fear or worry.

The *Law of Allowing* will manifest your desire if you let it. However, you must concur on this, that you are worthy and deserved to receive it. The best way to apply the *Law of Allowing* to you is to accept what is offered to you. (*For example, if someone offers you gifts or help accept and appreciate it. This will allow the Universal flow to continue and bring more abundance to you in your favor. It shows that you are telling the Universe you are appreciating and welcome the abundance.*)

The *Law of Allowing* is letting the energy flow easily to you without resistance. No resistant means you let go of control and let things happen to you naturally. Consequently, you no longer feel stress, fatigued and being alone, but with joy and happiness and recognize everything begins to emerge to you automatically and effortlessly. As of a result, everything you wish for has transformed and improved tremendously, and you live a healthy, productive, abundance life.

Finally, your strong belief will enable you to receive the many abundant events to happen to you, because the Universe has unlimited of resources and is yours for the asking. Always allow what is coming your way, accept it, and be grateful for your gift from the *Universe* and for what you have received.

Final Thought
~The Spiritual Laws of Success~

When you live with passion and purpose, and what you can imagine and believe can be achieved. You must believe beyond a reasonable doubt that your creative power in the latent subconscious mind is unlimited. The more success you achieve, the more prosperity and abundance you will enjoy. To facilitate greater wealth, you must develop a positive mental attitude and be focused to bring abundance into your life. So, you have set your creative power to attain all riches and wealth you desire to come to you now. You must clear away the negative influences that stand in your path to abundance, and implement the right course of action to achieve them. You understand only you alone can deliberately choose what kind of success you desire to bring into your life's experience. However, if you want real success you must align the power with the *Inner Source* to attain what you wish for. This is because a real success is hidden from within.

Here you are looking. Be proud of your success. Be happy of what you can do for one another. There are always so many things you can do to help, if you chose to do so. However, do it in good faith. Do not keep a hidden agenda in the conscious mind. If you approach the idea of helping others with a hidden purpose in mind and this will only discredit and deceive yourself.

Even though, on the surface the person that you are taking advantage of has suffered financial drawbacks, but at the end he is still a winner. You who are predaceous have only gained a shameful reputation to yourself because of your greediness.

We have heard people say money is power of all evils. It is false. It is wickedness when men violate and derail themselves and others by putting their selfish attitude first and not considering others and his actions. They employ their greedy minds target the wealth of other unconscious minds. They are the deceptive one, but not the noble money. This con artist approaches his prey with an agenda of helping and subsequently, gains the trust and faith of his victims. After gaining the trust and confidence of his prey, then he starts working on his plan. Unfortunately, these painful experiences always involve the glory of money. That is why money has a bad reputation. In fact, money is only a medium between men. Money has its value when bankers assign a value before the "0," this is true worth. Its acceptance can be denied when governments, bankers, and merchants declare the token money is no longer accepted and legalized as legal tender. Then, immediately the paper money becomes worthless. Money must be backed by Federal Reserve Bank in a country and normally in US currency. Money will lose its value and its time.

High influence energy will increase your self-confidence and awareness to bring wonderful things to enter into your life. You look after your body, mind, and spirit with good nutrition, diet and plenty of exercise, and most importantly, a positive thinking.

Because when you are vibrating higher energy you stay content and feel energized and powerful. The vibration of your desire and beliefs are in the same vibrational alignment. You can ask for anything to flow through your creative experience. You can look into your current situation right away to make a vibration match. When desires are met it indicates that you are feeling happy internally and everything is perceived inside and is very pleasant and peaceful. You glance at the external world it is full of kindness, caring, truthfulness, and also full of compassion and benevolence. You did not project to the external world and see jealousy, scam, violent, hatred, despair, confusion, and difficulties. Because in God's consciousness, that peace and love is observed. There are no struggles, unfairness, unfulfilled promise, and confusions in *His* consciousness. You will feel complete satisfied in God's world because it is where you come from.

Self-confidence leads you to act and speak with power and draws attention to come to you without effort. When your self-confidence is powerful, you can move mountains, because you are in the highest peak in your life. You can summon anything into your comfort zone. You have infinite success present to you. Your life is enlightened and empowered by your *Source*. Before you desire to do anything, you are always in a state that is connected to a higher energy field, with positive vibrational thoughts. You always carry the power of intent to the end and get impulse results. This magnetic energy adds vivid color into your life. Your life is full of fun, colorful and powerful.

You continue focusing on feeling this vibrating positive energy to meet with a new implemented thought and the desire to stay onboard and allow the energy to freely flow according to your personal preference. That is the power of thought energy acquiesces with your self-confidence and strong desire to succeed and live life fully and abundantly.

You can use the power of success to enhance strength or add to the desirable quality of your profession to run for higher position in the land. When you are powerful and confident and have the inner urge to do your desires you can't lose, but a strong desire to win. You show people that you can lead them to succeed in their paths. You are the ultimate winner because of the energy you vibrate resonate the power of your success and extend toward others, and from the truthiness of your heart.

Your self-confidence will shine on you and your soul appreciates you. This is because you always take the initiative in any situation without being held back. A person who has a leadership quality will always have the quality of integrity in his blood stream and the soul desire to do the ultimate best. Clarity of purposes is to unlock the gate and becomes the primary leader in your profession to do what's right for the soul.

When you are vibrating higher energy, you are more interested in life, than just living. You begin to engage in seeking your life purpose. You're willing to go the extra mile to do the research until you have the answer and the result.

You refuse to accept life is just stage. You believe there is something more than just living a standard life. The *Inner Source* has urged and drives you to seek more than just here and now. You have heard about spirituality, infinite beings, and the invisible source in the past. Now, you want to discover more about your real self and make conscious connection to this powerful spiritual Universe. You want to know what things really are and means to you. Because of your challenged personality, you start to question and begin to feel perplexed and puzzled. Many more unclear questions emerge regarding your life's purpose. You're unwillingly to just follow what other has said. You desire to seek the truth, nothing but the truth. Then, one day after prolong period of search and massive reading, you start to meditate for an answer and then you are awakened. You stop seeking for self because you have discovered the truth. A clear visualized picture emerges to indicate that your answer is obtained from within. The source is dwelling in your spiritual heart. Realizing your life purpose is carrying God's work on Earth. You are being sent here to fulfill God's assignment. Let your peers know about God's love and peace. Indeed, God is peace. Just look around everything created by God reflects His glory in many ways.

God dwells in your heart. It is a sacred place where you can take refuge and realize inner bliss, tranquility, and love. It is a hallowed place where you can realize your beigness. You see God's character by just look around. It transforms from your old beliefs to enjoy God, to receive grace, honor, and power, and give yourselves to be used for *His* purpose. Your life begins to improve, when you recognize *His* glory by loving *Him*.

Scientist visualizes their inventions in the mind before transforming into reality. We live in a dream land where everything comes to light through the power of imagination. The power of imagination is coming from the power of thoughts and to create a visualized picture in your subconscious mind and perceive success with the end results. It is a blissful person who has the quality of leadership; self-confidence knows how to apply the power of inner awareness towards any condition and situation to eliminate problems. The enthusiastic quality will lead him to succeed, because of strong emotions he knows enthusiasm has power to bring control into his life. He knows that balance in life is important. Let say enthusiasm is the feeling guiding him into action, while the willpower is the balance of your enthusiasm. When you feeling emotion you forget to control your mind without giving thought to your action, then you regret this and is too late.

A born leader knows how to implement the quality of his enthusiasm, exercise patience in the mist of turmoil and at the same time uses his self-control and enthusiastic abilities to make a quick and steadfast decision.

We have 60,000 thoughts or more every day in our waking hours, and many of our thoughts can work best for us. It is the minds strength that infuses the thought energy to direct the power of vibration to envision your creation. Thought is manifested by creating a visualize image in the mind to exert this energy outward and knowing that this thought moves from you to the *Universe* and expect it will return to you and your creation is manifested to affect the physical reality.

The bible version of forgiveness—love thy neighbor and thy enemy. In fact, this great book taught us to learn forgiveness and loves ourselves. Forgiveness is the healing journey for our body, mind, and spirit. It is meant for you and not for others. It does not mean reconciliation with the person that hurt you, or conditioning of their actions. But, it is inner peace that you hold onto any anger for too long in our minds. It is not only giving power away, but it is that we are simply hurting ourselves. Do not let other people's behavior stress you and drag you out of your comfort zone. Instead of focusing on your unhealthy feelings that are wounding you and giving the person who caused you pain power over you; learn to look for love and peace around you.

Holding forgiveness towards other persons will uplift the power of personal success and to improve your life. The only truth is to live your life successfully by sending love and peace to the physical world and meditate on God. This power will lead to success and enthusiasm for a truly compassionate life. Forgiveness influences our attitude, which opens our hearts to kindness and love. Our reality is the invisible light energy living within our physical body, which can be reached through the inner silence of the inner mind to begin to understand its ability and share its power and peace.

Our purpose here is to bring about the state of peace, harmony, and balance for everyone. Some people believe that we are allocated a spirit guide from birth. The best time to do this is just before bed time or before the waking hours and can be good time to communicate with the Soul, due to receptive state of consciousness existing at these times. Your spirit guide has chosen you and guides you.

However, the spirit guides are usually from the lower level of the Inner-Astral realm. You should always listen to your *Inner Voice*, who will know the true nature of the spirit guide, that you are in contact with.

The Source is actually the *Mind of God* and the creator of this physical world where we dwell. **The Source** is the most powerful high and only *He* can help you to achieve anything to meet with your heart's desire. All you have to do is meditate on God and constantly connect with **The Source**.

You pay attention to your inner state of consciousness. It is important to know you are attracting your own individual energy thought that is in harmony and vibrates to reflect your unique realities. Higher self-knowledge gives you the objectivity and the insight needed to clear your vibrational thoughts.

Jesus was asked, when the Kingdom of God should come, he answered, "the Kingdom of God is within you." (Luke 17:20-21) If the Old Testament says God is "I AM," what does the New Testament say? "God is love." (1 John 4:8; 16).

You are aware your physical body is composed of mind, body, spirit and is no secret that you are a spiritual being. Everyone can tap into the **Silence** of *Infinite Space* and feel the bliss and peacefulness in their hearts. However, every one experiences his/her unique connection to the knowledge within. You must experience and feel the silence from within, and then you know.

Mistakes and failures are unavoidable, but we need to admit and amend them, and avoid committing the same blunder again! Mistakes and failures hurt your personal experience, but only when you are thinking the most positive thoughts under any circumstance will help to eliminate doubt in its state to progress, improve the quality of your awareness, and know the true nature of your life. You are on the path of harmony and peace and in the ongoing process of managing your life and destiny. You listen to your *Inner Voice* to appreciate the significance and profound importance of this excellent advice, which are helpful and useful.

There are reasons, which cause failures because they help us to look further for answers. Everything happened for a reason and everything has happened for the best. Everything does happen and must happen, because this gap between failure and success can be amended by keeping your faith in yourself. So, if you give up because of failure you will never have the privilege of success again!

Practice truthfulness, benevolence, tolerance, and integrity will definitely enlightened your entire life and you reach the pyramid of fulfillment. When you meditate on these four reflective words you feel deepen the difference inside and outside. These words alone will nourish your soul and conscious mind to rise onto a new level. It enhances and uplifts your spiritual attitude and transforms your personality to greater success.

The great teachers use these four words as the basic principle in their teachings. Each word has very deep philosophical meaning on its own, which teaches us to live with harmony and meeting blissfully with each other.

You are inspired by these powerful words as you meditate on and project them to the physical consciousness, and knowing that is what you want to achieve and express your desires and objectives. When you really understand and master the true meaning of these prophetic words, and direct its power to penetrate the creative mind will be helpful, because it helps to cope with any situation in your life.

When, we meditate on the internal energy to hear its advice and to allow changing the external environment. In fact, we might forget the importance of these gentle urgings and know this will open us to new experiences, when we release of the external factors still influence us. In fact, both the external and internal are needed to consider what is possible and acceptable under the conditions of love.

Since we cannot compare these experiences with reality, then we might be comparing our experience with expectation. The fact is we cling to certain expectations and then we react with surprise to these events. These external factors (*For example, while you are in a book store rifling through books and suddenly a book falls in front of you. You realize this is the book you have been searching for and it contains the information that you need.*)

Often times, your prayer may be answered in an unexpected ways. You will receive whatever you ask for in prayer. When you ask you must believe and have no doubt because if you doubt your desire is blown and tossed by the wind. Therefore, you must believe your prayers will be answered from the *Universe* enables you to support to society and the joy is your reward. When you give generously, you have activated the *Universal Law of Giving and the Law of Receiving,* and the continual Universal flow of riches and wealth returns to you. You will find plenty of abundance and success and perfection abounding.

When someone gives you a gift accept it gracefully and you will attract more to flow to you. Accept this gift is a blessing from the *Universe* and attracts more beautiful things to come your way. However, if you refuse to accept a gift then nothing will happen, but you have placed a halt and telling the *Universe* to stop the flow of abundance to you. Sure you don't want this to happen.

Then, the spirit of giving and receiving know that this will lift you and others and is your condition of love. You offer it without any condition or feeling pressured. The decision is yours and is what you intended on doing and with no expectations of receiving anything back in return.

This is how often do you give to charity? You follow your intuitive feelings. I know you have given generously. Giving is a profound life experience. Every stage in life is unified by love and peace with each other and you are working within the scope of the *Universal Laws of Love.* Life is about abundance and harmony in your life's journey. People who do not understand this Universal Law is because of their limiting beliefs that they hold. But, you must recognize that we all share this innate power to help each other. Everything does happen for a reason. The *Mind of God* is what guides those events and allow them to happen.

It is similar to a hard drive in your computer. The files stored in the hard drive are separated into fragments. So, you need to defragment to put them back together in one place. It is very easy to do. All you need to do is apply software where it need be. Your hard drive will run smoother and better afterwards and it will appreciate you. However, human's life is unexpected. It changes all the time almost minute-by-minute and thought-by-thought. The moment you have put your life together and there will be always pieces left out unattended. These amazing surprises pop up to keep us organized and alert.

Life does not need to be this way and we should live life abundantly and wealthily without feeling scarcity. We are entitled to be wealthy and there is nothing wrong in thinking of being rich. It is the *Mind of God* who wants us to live in abundance and success. It is the flow of life and the Universals unlimited supply of natural resource that are granted to meet our every need.

However, how much money do we need to live large? There is no limit to living a wealthy life, because you replace doubt with thoughts of success. Unfortunately, we do know that our daily lives require the need of noble money to flow to us.

Because the ideas that you can live the full life and have faith that this abundant life is yours in the physical world. Money is a form of exchange for goods and services in the physical world. The paper money has no tag only when bankers and merchants agree to add value before the *zero*, and then the token money becomes the tool for trade and gross domestic product.

In the past, people say, "Money is evil." In fact, money is neither good nor evil. It is a symbol of power representing the true value of the exchange. Some people may not understand the true meaning about money. Money is your obedient servant and is internal. We need money for services, exchange for dwelling, health, and happiness. Money is a token value for the partnership with the world.

With it, it opens door to all sorts of opportunities and solves all our problems. However, if you are not mindful with money, it won't serve you right. You become a victim of your money because of your reckless attitude and misunderstanding of the value of money. There is no denial money represents freedom, independence, opportunity and the ability to do the highest good, as well as to fulfill hopes and dreams.

Before I started to write the content and body of my book, entitled *"THE AWARENESS OF MAGNETIC ENERGY"* I thought of the image for the front cover of the book. I imagined, what would be the best image to fit into the title of this book and achieve impulse results. The book is about applying the power of thoughts to attract to you the people, places, and references to aid in creating that successful and abundant moment and later transforms to become your own reality.

Immediately, I knew the eye is a good idea. I thought of it often until the desire developed. My confidents allowed me to transform the image into practical reality and become the front cover. I realize then the eye image attracted me. I could not imagine using any other image better than the "eye" because I believe it will catch everyone's attention. I believe it is perfect and serve the purposes.

You need positive thoughts, but not negative emotions. Sometimes an idea which is hurtful just come and goes. You acknowledge its presence and replace it with more positive attitude. Clarify your thoughts and ideas will eliminate any negative thought that cause confusion in the mind. When doubt is removed, then you can assert the power of your thoughts for what you desire. You have the power to summon the resources, but you must refuse to quit, determined to succeed and persistent it.

Everything is possible when you have faith and peace in yourself to move towards your desires and fulfillment, because you instill in your thoughts what you desire and how you envision your outcome.

You are the most valuable resource that you have in life when it comes to making the right decisions and choices, and you know what is good for you. Always avoid negative thoughts to eliminate unwanted energy when you making decision, and never let circumstance control you. You can choose the environment; select the people with whom you want to spend your time with and therefore your life.

When you are motionless attempt to empty your mind of being mindful and think of nothingness. Gradually, your conscious mind will separate the likes and dislikes and will bring thoughts that will only benefit you. Negative thoughts have a very deep-rooted connection to the past and can be terminated by practicing meditation and centering the mind. Meditating on love, compassion, and forgiveness will help you to cancel any negative desires emerging to you. Most importantly, give more time focusing on things that you enjoy and achieve faster and quicker. You must be vigilant, because lack of focus will affect the desire and is unable to continue and therefore you must light up your desire with absolute faith and invite the *Inner Source* to assist you. The power within will allow you to create a visualize image in your spiritual mind and is the starting point.

In its original state your thought forms a picture into formless substance to take shape through visualizing, or mentally perceiving it as you wish it to be, by joining with that specializing power in you is illustrated through the lens and later projected into the physical world. If your will is amply developed to hold your picture in thoughts and feelings without any disbelief and simply realize that your emotional thought is the conduit to attracting this power, then your formless image is certain to be projected onto the lenses, and transcend into the *Universe* and subsequently will return to become your physical reality.

If you can develop a habit of spending 25 minutes each day practicing meditation, will help you to resolve and have more lucid thoughts to promote good health and improving every aspect in your life. In the beginning of your meditation, do not force any surface thoughts out to disrupt you, but simply ignore them and it will opt out? With a strong mental will and your power of concentration will grow. Stop that little annoying thought, before they begin to take root and grow stronger.

Breathing exercises occupy the surface of the mind and allows you to concentrate on a deeper level. The longer you spend practicing in quietness; gradually you will notice the difference on how thoughts are emerging to you. The thoughts will become more tranquil, and peaceful.

Sometimes, it is difficult to contain negative thoughts penetrate into the mind, but if you make the effort to correct the imbalance to prevent it from happening again. Life is a balance and the key is to discover how positive and negative can change your life.

However, if you discover something is out of order, then it is your job to look within and fix it. You can perform this procedure by creating a vision to see through the subconscious mind to eliminate problems and amend those thoughts in order to change direction and you no longer feel the stress because you have released all suppressed feelings. If you want a truly happily life you need to release your suppressed feelings regularly and without hesitation. After you have eliminated all undesired feelings you can fully implement new beliefs that are more conducive to achieving.

In order to prevent and resolve your negative thoughts recurring to you regularly you can always find a solution within. If you consciously observed every negative thought carefully most of them are connected and related to your past and are echoing back to your current situation. However, you can cancel negative thoughts and re-direct your thoughts to a higher energy field, and by focusing on the intention originally desired. Finally, you must assess the challenges and possibilities and narrow your focus to reach your goals by using the strength of your inner thoughts and commit to the process until completion.

When you first set a goal to attract something you desire into your life you are fired up and ready to move forward at full speed. Your strong commitment, enthusiasm, encouragement and a good self talk in front of a mirror will boost your energy and feeling as if you just won a gold medal.

With the right attitude will help you to stay on track and to accomplish anything you desire. You must know how to make your goals a priority. You also need to build a strong foundation and belief in your abilities to reach all your initial priorities. You have to stay focused on your goals is vitally important in keeping your balance to prevent you from letting fear derail your efforts. The best method is to schedule a plan and stick to it.

It is also very helpful if you can create a visualized picture in your invisible mind and maintain this powerful focus to keep your intention alive. However, if your concentration is sharp and undisturbed the result will be much more effective. The stronger your thoughts are increases the ability you have to control every aspect of the creative process and this will lend to successful result you desires.

Everyone can fulfill their desires and manifest them in the physical world, but there are certain barriers in succeeding that should be taken into account. Any unsure mental activity and physical weakness caused by an ongoing illness can affect your determination and lead to confusion.

You have lost sight of your self-assurance, self-reliance, and faith, while you are waiting for the outcome. However, you must eliminate those negative emotional feelings should they recur, before you can reach any successful result. A steadfast attitude, focus, and patience are needed to achieve any successful result due to your vigilance, passion and your trust in your abilities to stay with it. It is quite natural for you to think of suspending your action, because you do not see the results coming your way or your visualization is not taking shape. You must realize your personal advancement depends on your personal power, whether you recognize you are at the center of your creation and connected with the *Universal Mind* within.

Therefore, do not feel discouraged and impatient, but exert a positive attitude, and continue to hold that creative image in the invisible mind and with a firm belief and commitment to carry forward your intention to unify the action needed to manifest the reality you want to see. This new expression and potentialities already exist within itself, if you allow this inwardly invisible energy to shape your thoughts will have an increase potential to reach any goal and solidify both outcome and condition needed to meet your heart's desire.

The exact directions given to the subconscious mind will bring all your dreams to light. However, it also takes a steady and continued action, and identifies the beliefs of your code, a fair judgment and self-discipline is also needed. Every day you gain momentum, as your inspiration deepens; it becomes easier for you to exert what you always desire to be, to have, and to do.

When you apply this energy of power to your subconscious mind, it is as your mind is connected onto a transmitter empowering your thoughts and ideas. Your vigilant thoughts become more affirmative about its intention and directives.

You must realize this inner power is purely controlled and facilitated by you. You can execute this inner energy to rejuvenate your physical body, mind, and spirit to fire up your energy. With this inner power embedded within you, you can continue enjoying what you do and feel relaxed, happy and fulfilled.

The power that governs this whole Universe can be tapped from within. However, you already have it. You want to communicate and learn from it. The *Inner Knowing* is a world of thought, feelings, and power and is full of life, love, and peace. It is invisible to the physical world, but its forces are powerful and noticeable.

The inner world is governed by the invisible mind. When you discover this inner world you will find the solution for all problems, the cause for every effect; and since the internal world is subject to your subconscious control, all powers and possessions are also within your control.

Faith endorses you with self-assurance and self-confidence to believe that you are also co-creator of this *Universe*. It is the strength of faith and belief in place and your emotional positive thoughts will give you the intelligence to see an inner vision and the practical skills to make this vision real.

Throughout history men learned that the more positive their thoughts were the better and the closer they were to center of their desires. While the more negative thoughts distance you from succeeding and accomplishing the goal and desire. However, whether you want to swim with the flow or go against the stream is in your power. When you decided to swim with the flow instead of swimming upstream, you will find that everything will fall into place, because you have stayed on course.

Positive or negative feelings come from thought impulses and are stored in the subconscious mind to either to be passive or active. The subconscious mind does not judge, but simply carries on what is recorded from your habitual thoughts and acting upon it accordingly.

Routine thoughts are thoughts that you think on regularly in your daily activities. With or without your knowledge some of these thoughts have contained negative impulses feeding into your mind unattended and continuously offering unhelpful impact and hinders your determination for success. Change and challenge yourself to become more responsible for your thoughts and actions.

A strong hold on ideas and determination are effective way to change and develop the way you perceive yourself in succeeding and living independently. You can eliminate and terminate all negative thoughts entering into the mind by upholding new value and directives to impress upon the subconscious mind to deliver what is best for you.

We all have this specific power stored in us. This thought power is coming through the Universe into your subconscious mind and you choose, which thought to form and create. After, your thought image transcends back to the *Universe* and ultimately returns to you with an impulse results.

Our vibrational thoughts penetrate into the mind two per second. Therefore, filter any negative thoughts that may influence your subconscious mind. The Universal law always works through the Mind of God and are sent from God. This power influences this planet Earth and aids the continuation of existence and the evolution of life to continue. It is the love of God that want this energy to flow forever and benefits every creature on the planet Earth. God promises will provide and send unlimited resource to us, so there is no scarcity and always enough for everyone.

Faith is the element of strong belief from within, which transforms ordinary vibration thoughts into miraculous events, created by us into the physical veracity. A person, who holds a strong faith inside, will stand firm beyond a reasonable doubt even in the middle of a crisis. He will refuse to accept failure, until the end and prevail over his torturer. Faith has created miracles throughout history and saved lives in the event of crisis's, turmoil, and despair. Faith is the connection between you, and God and the trust that the invisible *Source* of the *Universe* will bless you and deliver what is cast in your mind.

This person had experienced God's love and a miracle that saved him from turmoil because of his faith. Here is the amazing story he told me after the episode was over. This man was haunted by a human entity, and was hurt badly during one summer fifteen years ago. He was affected physically, mentally and spiritually by this incident. His hope was God would save and remove him from this severe situation. Because of his faith he had continued praying to God and hoping for the best. He had prayed for a week, then stopped praying and suddenly he experienced the calmness and peace from within that the *Infinite Universe* had felt his pain. He felt the unconscious part of him that knew his prayer was answered. He has faith in himself and faith in God. A miracle happened and freed him from this entity. Since then, he is more devoted to God and His love. His prayer had a strong pulling power and a stronger attraction to other similar thought vibrations that were joining it and becoming one powerful force in the *Universe*. As the thoughts momentum grew and combined with strong faith and imagination to slowly transform the objective into actual reality. It is accurate to describe this spiritual version of wisdom is within and his emotional thoughts has the task in mind and the strength of prayer using the five senses. At this highest spiritual stage the thoughts and feelings have conveyed and have impressed upon the subconscious mind to respond quickly and trigger his prayer to be answered and end the despair immediately.

You know that negative thoughts can disharmonize your mind and cause confusion. Your subconscious mind cannot distinguish between negative impulses can transmute them into veracity. All negative thoughts and plans are not desirable to hold in your mind and you should avoid hosting any of these negative impulses. However, only you can decide what you keep in the mind. It is your fate and no one can decide this for you. You must not let external forces determine and drive your life. If you want to live abundantly, you should fill your mind with positive vibrational thoughts and it will transform your fate.

You realize that any fear, doubt, and disbelief in the mind can cause a long or short-term side affect on you. It is a fact that these negative emotions can lower your vibrational energy, and you feel fatigue, temperamental, lack of self-esteem and uninterested in anything. However, if you don't want to be affected by these negative emotions, you can direct your thoughts to the higher energy field of a positive intention. The negative thoughts are the clear indications of your misalignment with the *Source* energy, but it does not reflect who you really are and what you really believe. As soon as you fill your mind with clutter, you have moved yourself away from love and peace, and down to the land of scarcity, misery, and failure. When you fill your mind with disbelief in your ability to connect with **The Source**, and the *Law of Magnetic Energy* will respect this and use this form of negative thoughts and then consequently, your subconscious mind will transmute these impulses into its physical reality.

Despite the uncertainty and doubtfulness in the mind you decide to swim back towards the current instead of swimming upstream, which will make things tougher for you. When you swim downstream you begin to feel everything becomes more receptive and clear, then you notice deep inside this urge to move towards this path and it is the right path. During this movement, you feel the water current is somehow different. However, it gives you a sense of inner calmness and that you must follow until the end. The current waves will lift you according to the way you set your thought to swim. Thus, when you find the right path and you listen, and follow the affects of your thoughts will empower you and open your mind to see a vision of faith and these are the real ingredients that influences your journey. There is a purpose for everything and your faith in your spiritual journey to reach **The Source** is not very much different, than the thoughts of love. In other words, your ideas, thoughts, desires, and the faith you have in yourself, which persuades the subconscious mind to bring anything manifested in the mental mind and transmute it into physical equivalent.

When you create your own aims in life, your subconscious mind activates and transmutes this into concrete reality. It is faith that gives positive thoughts vitality, life, and action. Faith is the direct element, which transform these normal thought vibrations by the conscious mind and manifested into physical equivalent. This is what many people refer to as *"good luck or good fortune."*

Your awareness of God will sustain your wishes, if you have mixed faith with your thoughts; the subconscious mind immediately picks up these energy and transforms it into actual reality. However, you must be aware that God helps those who help themselves first.

Imagine you want to create something you desire into your life. First step is to create a visualize image in your subconscious mind and you hold that picture until the time you feel confident enough to release this image and transcend it into the bountiful *Universe.* You must continually hold this image in a solid form in your mind and best mixed with faith, love, and emotion, that it instantly impresses the subconscious mind. It is the only form of action that persuades a response from the invisible *Universe* to transmute your desires into purposeful equivalent.

Your subsequent action must be taken into the material world to sustain the ability of thought impulses into its physical counterpart, love, health, wealth, or success. You believe in the power of desire to create positive thoughts and achieve your goals and your heart's objective. You must eliminate all clutter and negative influences and keep a lucid conscious mind, so that only positive emotional thoughts will enter into the physical mind to influence your desire. To achieve this objective you must determine to eliminate all old beliefs in your thought systems that you have accumulated over the years and re-programming new positive data into the mind. Your subconscious mind will continue recording data and the actions you carry out daily. Eventually, this new data will become a new habit in your emotional thoughts and as recorded in the subconscious mind and will obey and follow this new instruction. It will start bringing you new energy, since it is the only single positive thought being recorded and will sustain this into reality.

Re-programming new thoughts or ideas into your mind, first off you must understand clearly what you desire. Your clarity of thought has brought you new creative concept into your mind. Then, you proceed to implement this new idea to override your old thoughts that are no longer sustained by you. After, you program this new idea into your environment, let it automatically supersede any negative emotional feelings and immediately replace them with the positive emotional thoughts.

You understand thoughts are vibrational energies coming from the invisible *Source*. When energy is vibrated with positive emotions it has created an alignment with *The Source* through the subconscious mind. However, you must continue being vigilante to implement new ideas and navigate to harmonize with *The Source*. If everything is in harmony with your new thoughts and you'll accomplish your objectives through the act of faith and your desire will be carried out.

When you are focusing your mind on a desire to create what you really want, you know the feeling of joy and blissfulness from within is connected to your vibration impulse and is now triggered and will be sustained by the *Mind of God*.

A feeling of enthusiasm shows that there is a very strong desire at that moment and you know that your thought energy is in alignment with the *Inner Source* and is directing this power to **The Source.** When you are thinking of abundance, you eliminate any other thought of lack. You are only considering one specific thought in the mind to override any intruding contradictory thoughts. However, you mix faith, love, and emotions with your desire. Thoughts mixed with faith and love constitutes for this magnetic force, and attracts other related thoughts. Your sole thought will prevent negative feelings from entering into the mind that may otherwise complicate and affect any desired result. When you really want something you must navigate your thought towards your accomplished goal and allow only positive energy into the mind. Your vibrations are an indicator of your contentment. They help you to know whether you are closer to your fulfillment.

You don't need to contain negative thoughts, but reject them as soon as possible before they emerge. You can always redirect your thoughts back to the original idea and intention, and carry on your work. Do not allow any depressing emotions to interrupt your focus on one powerful thought. Remember, the thought that you send to the *Inner Source* from your conscious mind must have the same vibrational match with the subconscious mind and to harmonize with the *Mind of God* and that energy will flow to get the results.

We create our own thoughts and conditions to live independently. You have a choice to live in either in the Now or continuously in the condition of the past, which has no merit. It is only you alone that can make this decision, and nobody can decide this for you.

You are the creator of your own life and have the power to create a new desirable environment. Signs and symbols are everywhere for you to observe, which one will appeal to you and suit your needs.

The new implemented idea and dominating thoughts will manifest themselves internally first and are projected by you to the external condition and gradually transform them into physical reality to make changes in your life. However, if the conditions you focus on are wealth oriented, your thought of faith has helped to bring the right emotions to be sent to **The Source**. Then, this thought you have sent to the mind will tell you that the *Inner Source* realizes your request and your preference will return to fulfill your desires.

You will feel a moment of joy when your desire is in the process of moving towards you, you are experiencing blissfulness and peace. In addition, there will be many opportunities for you to prepare, evaluate, decide, and enjoy your creation.

I want you to know you hold the power and control to experience your own desire. Concentration can help you to strengthen your creative power in the manifestation field. Before you decide what you wish to manifest and write down a list of your accomplished goals. It helps you to create a habit of doing things. It tells the subconscious mind this is your daily routines. A positive message is sent to the latent subconscious mind so that there will be no misunderstanding or misalignment, only balancing from within. When the energy is transcended to the *Universe*, the energy that connected to **The Source** is the same as received and is recorded in your subconscious mind will begin to bring everything you desire.

However, it is important that you continue to be aware of the positive thought energy and be focused on the impulse within you and block all negative unhealthy influences to enter into the mental mind that may have subsequent impact on the final result of your desire.

Nature gives us free will to do what we want and to think freely without limitation on our thought patterns and any dissimilar thought which could disrupt our freedom to create new thoughts. However, you must filter your vulnerable thoughts to achieve your objective, because allowing negative thoughts to penetrate into your mental mind will affect the subconscious mind and delay processing your request and translate negative results to you. This is because the subconscious mind does not ask, but just fulfills the order submitted by the mental mind. It is very important for you to know the relationship of the subconscious mind and its mission to bring you where you desire to be, and to do.

In the past, we did not acknowledge the power of the subconscious mind to bring us these creative impulse thoughts. We did not reach out to the subconscious mind and influence it with our positive thoughts. Instead of seeking help from within we look to the external world for assistance, and we were disappointed. We are not able to achieve what we desire because we keep omitting the truth and looking outside of ourselves for our answer and expected desire. Until one day we are awakened and realized that our desires are manifested from within before it gives birth to the physical world and then we know. From then on we know our abilities to manifest our desires is from within. Therefore, we must recognize our power is obtained from within, but not acquired from the physical world.

You must be aware of your inner power before you can achieve anything you want in the physical world. Without knowing the power, the wisdom, the intelligence, the strength, the faith and the enthusiasm instilled in you is found from within, but your freedom of creation is limited.

Life continues to unfold and what is given to you in the physical world is the power of the knowledge from within. You must also recognize our objectives are processed through the subconscious mind to link up with your conscious thought and connect with your infinite soul, where everything comes to light.

We are living in a fast-track communication age where information can be obtained easily and rapidly through the internet and other knowledgeable sources. Knowledge helps us to improve the quality of life, intellectual ability, needs and wants will transform.

Because of technologies advancing this aids to improve the effectiveness and functionality of the mind through the refinement of communication skills. Whether you chose to use this adaptation or take the next step in the progress of your life depends on how adoptive you are. It is your denial of truth that you do not want to live higher quality of life. We all want to live abundantly without feeling lack or having financial challenges all the time. In fact, everyone deserves to live in the Land of Abundance but not in the Land of Lack. However, you can change your perception of what you are conceiving by mediating on the desires from within.

You can go further by asking the Divine to assist you to achieve the peace within you. When you can heal yourself by seeking help from within then the abundance will begin to emerge into your life and draw helpful people to come to you automatically and effortlessly.

The healing power is gained from within to heal painful experiences over the years and you may not even be aware or notice them. These painful experiences know your weaknesses and occasionally emerged to you unexpectedly like an express train approaching the platform without warning. When you did notice it was already in front of you, it was too late to avoid it. However, these unpleasant past events and experiences can be shut off in your conscious mind by healing yourself. It is very powerful when you can follow this healing procedure to heal yourself. Remember, no one can do this healing for you, but yourself. It is an action you should not take it lightly. It is for the benefit of your body, mind, and spirit. In the long run, it heals you completely and eliminates worry or fear, to terminate the past, which may come back to haunt you. However, you only need to do this procedure once then it is done. But you must believe beyond a reasonable doubt that this will works well and speak for itself.

I know this experiment worked very well because I have tested it on myself. It healed the inner problems I held in the past and they are no longer an issue. I recognize this healing procedure is very powerful and everyone can do it. In my personal experience for example, I pulled out a picture of a particular person.

Then, I called on the Divine Light Power to help and guide me. I said to the picture, "*I am sorry; I hurt you for what I had said and done in the past. Please forgive me and I love you. Thank you.* " All of sudden, I felt a heavy emotion being released from me. The person I am with, in this picture has deceased in the year 2005. I regretted I did not have a chance to say good-bye or pay tribute to him. I felt inner guilt, but I could not do anything about it and beyond my power. Anyway, I repeated the metaphor until I calmed down and felt the peace within. At the time, I was very emotional and did not realize it had such a great healing impact on me. I did it to heal my body, mind, and spirit. Now I am glad I did and to heal this long due pain. I feel great from within. This is so powerful because I have indeed healed the suppression within. As soon as I did this, I have released and accepted the conditions that led me to this powerful change. It is a permanent healing which is empowered by the Divine to assist me in the healing process.

You can try this and gain your own experience. However, you may need to substitute a different metaphor to meet your situations and circumstances needs to see the ultimate healing results. The effectiveness of your healing outcome will certainly amaze you. You are using your own source power to heal others as well as yourself because you are one source and meet with the void. Every day after using this practice, you realize that life is full of Divine abundance, but is very alive and active. It is connected with beating hearts and souls. It is a beauty of life.

I want to elaborate more on the use of metaphors, so that you can see the effectiveness of applying this to your own situation. For the best result you need to endure and use imagination and emotions to assist the power of intention to achieve and get results. Emotional feelings are needed to impress the subconscious mind you mean it. The subconscious mind will only act on with pre-define instruction and will not making any changes. Therefore, whatever you submit to the subconscious mind will process, be stored, and recorded in the database. When the data is requested, the subconscious mind will retrieve the information and send it back to the conscious mind. A merely to say word by word is not good enough to make any changes you intended to do. You need to break your old habit barriers so that your thoughts will be coordinated with your real intention that you want to carry out. You must allow the power of your thought words to align with the subconscious mind and let your conscious mind act upon the directives creative power to amend any of many barriers holding you back. It is like a second skin engraved inside your mind and the subconscious understands you want to carry on and working from there. The signal is a direct imprint into the subconscious and is therefore very powerful and effective way to guide and manifest your wish directly.

Every step in the process you may find difficult and confusing because of your old habits and beliefs, making it difficult to manifest any changes, but all you have to do is swim with the fold instead of swimming upstream and otherwise you will never see changes in your life.

It is like living in your comfort zone for so long whether it is painful or comfortable and you could not distinguish from them unless you have determined to jump out of your comfort zone and see the new changes emerging into your life. Change is good because it transforms your life to a whole new level and to discovering what you want to see and go where you want to go and to do what you desire.

Don't be afraid to see transformation occurring in your life, because life should not be in one pattern of thought, but should be evolving all the time. You deserve to have joy and bliss in your life, but you need to change your thinking pattern to receive the abundance and prosperity and those changes will lead you to transform your feelings. Eventually, your life will take on a whole new meaning and you will be glad you took a step forward.

Energy offers variable source of power. When energy flows without resistance we become super magnet conductors. Free from any restriction and resistance, it is very easy to achieve our desires without effort. If you think of goals, you want to accomplish immediately your encounter thoughts that will stop you and your body gesture sends out a signal of feeling angry, frustration, fear, and doubt. Any feeling that is not positive will empower resistance.

Resistance stops the flow of energy and is the cause of stress. When resistance emerges, it halts all actions. Even though you manage to take some action, but ample amount of energy must be applied to enable an action to take place. At the end, you are feeling exhausted and wish to give up.

However, there are solutions to your existing problems by exercising non-resistance. When you are not resisting you know what you desire to do, to be, and to receive and you are able to do it faster. Without resistance, there are unlimited resources and abundance and easy to see a clear picture. You have plentiful choices and opportunities to obtain your goals and get things done without pushing the limits.

In fact, in truth there is no problem. The problems that you have encountered are feelings of confusion and making them real. You believe it and become your own reality. Feelings are emotions that have disrupted your progress because you have followed your negative thoughts. You see the truth as in your mind and experiencing the desire outcomes and feeling it. You probably experienced when there was a time in the past you want something very much, but you did not have it. However, when you are not contemplating on it, then it emerges to you and made you very happy. Because there is no resistance and everything comes naturally. You have surrounded your resistance power to **The Source** and feel more relax and liberated.

Do you know there are difference between the term "I want" and "I have?" Let's assume that you are thinking of wanting to buy a car, immediately you have a counter thought of scarcity. Where do I get the money? Where are your emotions? However, if you change you're thinking patterns to you have possession of that car and seeing it emerging in your possession shortly.

Then, you have acquired and acknowledge you have the ability and the creative power within you to produce the desire results because you are not thinking of lack, and believe you shall have it soon. This released your limitation of feeling lack. You know you will own that car very quickly.

You have opened unlimited resources, and they immediately become available and you feel confidence in knowing it will become your own reality.

Now you have learned that there is no problem. The only problem is created in the mind. The mind has created that resistance preventing you to have prosperity, wealth, and good health. However, after you have released what you want and replaced this with image of the object in possession and believe you will have it soon. Then, you simply let go and it will send a signal to the subconscious that your thinking and feelings are in alignment to bring with this vibration harmony and consciously connected with **The Source** and believe your wish will arrive to you. You have activated your plan to receive what you're wanting. This will enhance the energy of your physical body, mentally and spiritually. You feel more relaxed, joyous and blissful, and preparing to receive what you desire to have in your possession and feel the peace from within.

Are you aware there are things that once you thought you couldn't do, but now you can? At one time I thought I couldn't write, but now I can. I have completed a titled book, *The Awareness of Magnetic Energy*. In fact, everything is possible if you believe you can.

The things do not change, but you must change your mind to make room for achievement. It is the desire in your mind and determination to transform the matter into reality and does not matter how impossible it may sound in the past, but is achievable with your belief. You have transmuted the idea of your belief system and recognize the world from within and when comparing to the faith and belief you have now.

You see the problem do not exist in the external world, but within yourself. You do not recognize who you really are and thought that your abilities are limited. Your old beliefs limited you to what you can and can't do. However, when you change the thinking patterns of your belief system to seek the truth and you will find the truth of your world is from within. The external world is full of struggle and challenge, unlike your world within, is full of peace, joy, and blissfulness. Therefore, when you seek from within so shall you receive the truthful answer to your problems? Then, you realize the ability is given to you to work with your Inner Source, but not the external world. As soon as you change the idea of your thought it will transform anything you believe in will become possible.

You have a choice as what to feed into your mind or what you can or can't do. You also have a choice of how to condition your mind to accomplish challenging tasks and to reach the pinnacle in your life. You determine what you are going to write in your book and no one can make that decision for you. You need to be aware that life is like acting on the stage. However, what script you use will feed into your life and descriptions of the play that you are willing to experience.

Whatever script you write will reflect your situation in the conscious and is used by the subconscious to impress upon you to carry it out. Indeed, you are the only person, who can control the horizontal and the vertical and no one can take control for you. You are the only person who can ultimately change it by conditioning your mind to positive thinking. You have the power to create the real you and experience what life has presented to you by taking control of your thought and to change your life.

Your thought is spiritual energy and is carried to you through vibration. The power of your thought is transformed to form through formless. When the energy is created and vibrated with the Law of growth and the Law of Love and it will return to you.

However, you need to have a healthy mind, body, and spirit to carry the task you have contemplated in the mind. It is our desires to express freely and harmoniously without holding onto everything in us. Anger, frustration, and jealousy can be eliminated when you know yourself well. It is true that one has the power to control and eliminate any undesirable thought entering into the mind and holds the power to control to his fate and destiny.

The strengths and powers to purify your thoughts will defy worrying energy to enter into your mind. Your calm attitude will bring peace to the mind as the situation arises and then you can handle this rapidly and easily. Thus, a creative and effective thought is an important process in your growth and knowing how to apply them.

The power of success is from within you and your rights to acquire it. You don't need to admire other people success because you have the ability within. Success is not limited to the privileged mogul and famous. New opportunity will open upon for you if you have faith in yourself to accomplish what it is you desire, but you must know where to look. Sometimes, it is necessary to shift your belief system in order to receive your goals. The Universe of opportunity will flow to you forever with unlimited resources, if you know how to take advantage of them.

The Inner Source is the aspect of your thought vibrations, is found within to experience the inner harmony, beauty, and love, and although, you can't perceive it, but its forces are ultimately there and are powerful. Behind the secret of manifestation is your expressed thought through the emotional feelings connected to spirit and your creative expression and strong conviction that you are ready to receive it? Your strong commitment will break all barriers allowing you to link between the Universal Source and the subconscious to bring vibrational harmony to reach your heart's desire. Your desire gradually, transforms everything to form from formless and ultimately, return to you with an impulse results.

When you can express your desire freely in a mental level this allows you to let the energy of your thought to flow freely and having faith in the ideas forth coming in your mind. You hold on to this concept in the mind and you will automatically attract the attention of the Universal Law of Magnetic Energy to bring that choice to you and to manifest with desired results.

One must allow one's desires to be fully expressed to live freely in life. An unexpressed or unfulfilled dreams and desires will lead to complication, confusion, and unhappiness. Things will stand still and the feeling of the blues and pressure emerges upon you unless a revolutionary breakthrough helps you to express your desire and leads to victory and completion. You will stay where you are until your expression is fulfilled, and then we will never experience sadness and feeling disposed. One's expression is defined "*when a person dreams and desires are fully fulfilled and expressed, there is a feeling of completion and satisfaction and has nothing left to be undone and he can die happily.*"

Every aspect in your journey on Earth, you have an invisible guide with you, that leads you through to fulfill your purpose. This invisible source is omnipresent and ready to help you. You may not be aware of it, but it is present. Every event happen is for your learning experience, which helps to improve your knowledge and empower conscious awareness.

When you change your mental thought through the lower consciousness, you have also influenced the changes in the spiritual level. Seeing both the spiritual and the mental consciousness is joined in vibrational harmony, which is integrated to hold and the achieve impulse result. It is the invisible force of consciousness awareness, which holds that thought into its own experience and when the consciousness has connected to this experience, its existence is in the past and is cancel by the mind.

Therefore, everything happens is originated through the power of thought, which is observed in the spirit level and subsequently transforms the thought energy into the physical form and becomes potentially effective reality.

Therefore, our inner power combined with thought joins with the Universal Mind of God. Because in the beginning there was the word and this was the expression of God. It is through the powerful expression of the Mind of God that everything comes from formless to form. It is through the power of faith in us and the connection with the Mind of God in spirit to convert everything to physical substance and back to you.

Creating the reality in your life is within you. You must be in the moment to perceive the future. In fact, the moment you think of a thought was already the past and the future has already arrived. Therefore, what you are thinking right now will have a profound effective towards the next moment. In other words, your thoughts and ideas of what you are thinking of doing will reflect the joy, happiness, abundance, success, and experience in each moment. It is important to stay in the moment and stay connected to your future plan.

Here is something you will find very interesting and refreshing to your body, mind, and spirit. Recently, I learned to give thanks and love to almost everything, every organism, and non-living thing. Giving love to the home and including the empty space will return blessings to you.

Talk to the empty space within and ask how it feels thus far. Feel the response from the empty space. Tell the empty space you love it and hope that the empty space feels joyful and peace also. Nonetheless, you let the empty space know you love it and enjoy their company and presents.

I know it may sound weird and uncomfortable to do this. However, in fact it is very natural and brings peace into the surrounding. If you are aware of everything is made of energy and energy is power. Power has active forms therefore it contains positive or negative. It is like doing a ritual cleansing in your home on the solstice of spring. It shows that you respect everything that the Divine has created and provides you with everything in your living environment. Indeed, you want to continue feeling the joy, love and peace that dwell with you and although you can't see but you can feel it. You send the space a message that you are happy and feel the love and joy fills the room and in return the room will appreciate you, too.

While I was writing the above message, I received a profound message from **The Source**.

Behold, I love you, I love you, and I love you. You are not quite completely quiet in your mind. You need to observe what is presented to you from above and so below, and follow the direction that always benefits and inspires you. Feel the silence and clarity of thought to catch my thought in you. You must not worry too much. You are indeed worrying too much at the moment. Trust and faith must fully develop to integrate learning to hear "MY" voice in the silence.

Thus far, you may not see where it comes from and where it is going. Things will be taken care of and becomes transparent soon. There is no direction or destination indicating how to receive the right answer, but listen from within. Tranquil your mind, connect from inspiration and then you know what to do. Clean up your past memories and programs preventing from being you. You accept what is happening as happening. All you have to do is to accept the moment. Remember this message is from **me**, *but not from memory. By saying "I love you" you have allowed yourself to connect back to* **me**. *Though you may not be aware of it, but you know I am love. It is the origin* **The Source**, *I am. As you learn from inspiration, you will not rely on what you have recalled, therefore you find insight. Clarity of your thought and wait for an answer. You will understand why you are involved in this external happening in the accelerating world and share the experience. I know you are worrying about lot of things still, but let me remind you do not need to worry and the transmutation of things shall improve. You must allow time to demonstrate and show you what has occurred through* **me**. *You deserve enriched life while you are dwelling on Earth. Remember* *to remove any unnecessary thoughts that keep you from living abundantly. Your book is part of "My" will and "My" power has endorsed and blessed it. You must feel the love and peace from within in order to bring love to others through the awareness of your innate ability. I am the one who has inspired you to write this book, "THE AWARENESS OF MAGNETIC ENERGY." Therefore, when you follow my direction and guidance then everything will thrive and will be abundant. You deserve everything for your hard work and the success is within you.*

You must believe to receive and then see it in your own reality. All is well for you and you can't fail by applying the potential and the unlimited power and its will within you. The truth of success rests in your heart and soul. The secret of success lies upon the love and service to others. I stop here now so you can contemplate what I have just said to you and until next time is well. I am.

Now, my positive attitude and the confidence have sustained me to carry on writing with the aid from The Source. I deny and defy any negative thoughts and I am resting my knowledge on my Inner Knowing, and its will that is within me. My thoughts become more lucid and coherent. I am bridging between my spirit and The Source that I am receiving these signals, as if data emitted by radio transmitter so that I can receive, translating them into words.

Your individuality is who you are and how you represent and present yourself in a particular way that shows your attitude and aptitude with the relationship with I am. The aptitude is what you know, attitude is feeling the peace from within, and I am God from within.

When you are giving and did not expect a return and everything will come to you. You have to open yourself to the goodness and greatness of the Divine. The Divine is in the body of you. Success is within the physical and the spiritual self. You will succeed, only by creating to serve others with a selfless heart and trust in others. The true fortune in life lies in the devotion to God.

Your success is based on the expression of knowledge, when feelings and emotions are in touch with the endless spiritual richness of **The Source**. You will realize your outward potentials are limited and you turn inward looking for wisdom and wealth and trace the feelings and emotions coming from within. You are your own source. When you purify your thought with unconditional acceptance and love and your trends are the awareness of what you intend on implementing and can lead to contentment, happiness, and balance and inner peace.

Success is manifested from the Universal Law of Nature; you believe you already have enough and more will come to you. You help people to succeed with a selfless heart, it is God, who wants you to succeed, and His will bestows blessings upon you from Heaven. Success is learning from experience and allows for transmutation. Success is from inspiration, but not from memory. Success has created a visual image in your mind's eye into form from formless, and transcends it into the Universe and holds that thought and later becomes your own reality. Success is when you know what you desire to have and know. You have already perceived a vision of what you determine to have and believe you shall receive it shortly. You must always focus on what you have instead of what you don't have. You must be detached from everything and do not be concern too much or in control of the outcome. Faith plays an important role in manifesting your dream and many portals will open to you. In your belief system, you must believe beyond reasonable doubt and feel the peace in you to receive your heart's desire.

You must accept this as true that God wants you to succeed and He will provide and supply you with every need to succeed and be successful. Your maximum success is service to God and sharing your fortune, and generosity.

You desire to achieve your ultimate success in life is from inspiration, but not from a recurred theme. You listen quietly to **The Source** say to you and follow through. You cannot fail; because you will be guided by listening to the rhythm of **The Source** who inspires you, but does not come from what you experience externally from your past. When you rely upon experiences in the previous screen of events, it confuses and upsets you. Often times, we failed because of the preceded events reminds us of our memories and are afraid to attain it again. It hurts us every time we recall from memory and therefore it is not reliable and does not sustain your needs. Acknowledge them and be grateful of what you have and then act on whatever inspires to take action.

Most importantly, you have a clear-cut vision of what you desire to have and believe this will come. It is because in your beliefs system you know very well that your desire can be transmuted into its physical equivalent!

It is also important for you to know and to keep that faith and hold the desire in your imagination and your persistence are the real ingredients that guide you to your pursuit and feel the outcome of what you do. It is faith you have conveyed in the mind and becomes the significant success of your idea!

Success begins in the form of thoughts. Thought is the medium influencing the subconscious mind to obtain an impulse result. It is the agency of dominating thoughts, which bridges between the mind of the conscious and the subconscious mind to be activated by vibrational thoughts.

However, whether these thoughts are positive or negative is immaterial, because you will achieve auspicious results.

Nature is very fair to men, that he has control over the material thoughts, which reaches the subconscious mind through the energy power of the five senses, emotions and feelings and men have always had the control of these powerful thoughts.

Remember that the subconscious mind is like a fertile garden spot, weed will grow in the abundance soil, if seeds of more desirable crops are not sown properly. The same principal applies to the conscious thoughts of creativity or the destructive nature, which you voluntarily permitted them and let them find the way to feed into the rich garden of the mind.

For example, if you want to manifest your money consciousness in your thought impulses. A mere reading out loud of a statement will not help you to manifest the effect you want to produce. You need to add an emotion and feeling mixed with your spoken words and your subconscious mind recognizes and acts upon these thoughts which are blended with emotional feelings, strong faith and belief. Fail to do so you will receive no desirable results.

For example, I intend to manifest 30,000$ for the purpose of meeting needs of others and the service it extends to me and the world around me. Now it is done and so it is. Thank you. Then, pay attention to your desire in the Universe; the spirit realm will guide you to manifest that specific amount of money emerging to you. Because you attract what you desire and we give our energy to what we drawn to us. Thought energy causes sensational and emotional feeling in your body therefore it is important to maintain the state of positive vibrations in the mind. And the *Law of Magnetic Energy* initiate what is transcending to the *Universe* and flows back all that is related to your intention and becomes your own reality.

Now what can you do to transform your desire into actual reality? When you desire something or your intention determines the level of energy to focus your inner power to receive the desire effect. The more energy, confidence, faith and steadfast you are, you then draw upon your inner power to keep your desire focus and alive, and will allow for room to let this happen. Again, you must be aware of what your desire is about. If you desire is to lose weight in three months, then you have to monitor and modify your diet or bring methods in the ways that are for the highest good and flows to you in a steady, unbroken and increasing stream of success and good health. The moment you choose to feel more and more confident in manifesting your desire, it will shape the success of your destiny.

One thing you should not get disappointed, if you cannot direct and control your emotions the first time to get what you desire. Remember you need to set your expectation and keep focused on what you really want to manifest by applying the power of intention and the connection to spirit of the Universe. The ability to influence your subconscious mind is by applying the powerful force of persistence. You must decide whether you pay a price for your effort. Your ability to succeed in manifesting what you desire depends, upon your power of concentration and the power of intention and a given desire until that desire becomes a burning obsession.

The subconscious mind will take into fact anything sent from the conscious mind with good faith. You need to repeat and present your desire repeatedly with no doubt, but a strong commitment and act upon the recurring idea that you desire to manifest.

You probably want to change your life in a most profound way and the shortest and easy way to receive the abundance and wealth is by limiting any complicated law and confusion in the mind. You want to apply a single method without going into precise details and to follow simple guide lines and use the sub-detail of the Universal law to obtain the things you desire.

In today's accelerate world what is about to emerge has already happened and must occur. You realize that there is nothing in your power that can stop it from happening. These invisible forces are governing the whole Universe regarding how and when everything shall emerge to the physical realm.

However, you don't really need to know how it happens, but be ready to receive them, should they emerge to you, be still in silence to hear the clues from the Universal Mind as to how you should act and prepare for your inspired life. All you need to do is trust, believe and receive the Universal flow of increasing stream of wealth, prosperity and success.

If you choose to believe in a prosperous and abundant life that is exactly the life you will experience. However, if you believe nothing is going to go your way, then you experience a black cloud hanging above your head and overshadow you at all time and that black shadow shrouds your thought with doubt and fear will most certainly be there if unchecked. So what kind of life you choose is up to you.

From inspiration you choose to decide to be more and more confident and believe you have the power in choosing the right action. You take immediate action to let go of your undesired habits and stressed out conditions. Invite and allow the *Divine Light Power* to assist you in making the right decision and the invisible force of *Universe* is inspiring you towards the right direction.

Now you perceive that all problems are removed and replaced with love, peace and joy which are reflected from the inner state of mind to the world without.

Now silence the mind to imagine all your problems have been released. Think of the moment that make you feel joyous and blissful. It could be the moment you have begun a most rewarding and successful journey in your life.

You travel back in time to your graduation date and you have all these joys and happiness on your face. The moment of joys and happiness are engraved in your memory and record in the subconscious mind. Now think of the people, events and circumstances that brought you where you are now with success, wealth and fame. These are positive events that you choose to keep and continue to desire them. At this moment continue to hold that positive vibration thoughts, but you jump back to the Now. Think of everything you have desired and received naturally, automatically and effortlessly. You feel miracles have happened to you and feel fortunate and blessed. You have discovered over the years, all your specific desires have transformed into actual reality and the outcomes are as good as you wanted it to be. Every day, in every way you are getting healthier and wealthier. You feel grateful to the Universe sending you these great gifts simply just ask and be given. You give thanks with gratitude. You appreciate the great power of the invisible *Universe* for the abundance and wealth. You contemplate the many great reasons you should show your gratitude. You are thankful for many wonderful events and unlimited quality of wealth that has happened in your life. You give thanks to the great *Universal Mind of the Universal Creative life Force* for wish granted. Before you understood, you must understand only with a grateful mind that will manifest everything to your heart's desires.

You believe there is good in everything that happens to you in the present. That's how your life will unfold and making the choice is your decision. It is something that you can influence. It is the current moment or simply calls the *NOW*.

When you are in the present moment you will realize there is nothing to worry or fear about, but peace and harmony. It is the silence in you that you feel the inner peace and joy. Because you're constant choice for genuine change in the present moment automatically cancels the need for a better you in the visible future. You are doing better now is all that really matters! With this positive attitude you are now being re-directed to a higher energy field instead of swimming upstream and beware of your infinite being as the true source of prosperity.

So, how your dream transmutes into actual reality does depend on how and when you want to settle your goals.

Let me illustrate one example here:

I want a bigger dream home.

Now be very specific and add more details: I want to move into my dream home with two-storey, a basement, a den, a fireplace, and a Japanese landscape and waterfall on _____ or by December 1, 2009.

See how specific goals are!

Goals are inclusive and a deadline are particular important. Plans without particular date or deadline are unclear when the event will actually happen. Therefore, it is easy to get stuck into "*someday*" in a person's mind. And oftentimes "someday" may not even occur. In other words, I have my dream home "soon" or may never happen because of my ambiguous mind. It is like when I will see you again! Soon! When? Soon! Oftentimes that particular vague promise does not occur, because the event will never happen due to uncertainty. So, reconfigure your thoughts and clarifying your dreams and goals into more specific details so the events will occur. It will clarify your dreams and desires, and transform goals into physical reality and quicker than your thoughts.

Is it not a time for you to unleash…and begin to get what you desire in your life? It is never too late to start. The Universe has plentiful "*ABUNDANCE*" to share with everyone and is always there waiting for you to claim possession. You determine the kind of success you want to manifest, place it in the manifestation field and the success is within reach with a positive vibrational thought.

Most importantly, you can't just sit there waiting for this to happen. Your idea must follow with the best action. Without bringing your thoughts into actual action, then nothing will happen. Dreaming is good, but a dreamer must be able to transmute his dreams into his own reality. He can't lose, but only success will befall upon him and being blessed with abundant life.

You have the power to rewrite your own reality. It is not difficult and you must be willing to make that transformation, because the determination and power is within you to see improvement and accomplishments in your life. One of the easiest ways is to change your beliefs system and look into your thought patterns to transform your life. Once you have adopted a new belief system you will see many improvements and radically change your life. You will attract many good things you are longing for and the people, events, and conditions needed to amplify and create the world you will see around you.

For example:

Every day, in every way I feel strongly that I am living in the land profoundly fill with health and wealth.

Every day, in every way I believe and feel more and more confident that I have manifested success and wealth in my life.

I have succeeded in everything I touch and enjoy it. I have achieved what I wanted to accomplish and become one of the wealthiest men in the globe. I find contentment in myself because of the connection to the self and God. I feel joy and happiness dwelling in me. I feel God is everywhere and feel his presence within me. Success and abundance is a limitless resource coming from the invisible Universe.

Transformation takes place when you begin to see a newer you. You become a teacher from a student. Your seed of growth become more mature and full of *Divine light* to express abundance and success. You already know how to seek for your insight from within and balancing the thought in your soul. You know profoundly the significance of seeking the richness is from within. It is, as a tree needs water, sunshine, and nutrition to grow stronger and begin transformation. You can overcome your greatest challenges through the connection of your ideas and hear the voice from within. You can develop a practice of setting a date and time to recognize how to develop a plan for success in helping people around you and the balance you want to achieve in your life. You have to surrender and let go of control and have complete faith and trust in life. You have to surrender to spirit to achieve your goals. Without fully surrendering to God, it is difficult to accomplish your success. Once you surrender you begin to develop the evolution of insight and make changes in your attitude and adopt new ideas to implement that change you wish to see.

You must be patient. You need to give more time for everything to cultivate, to extend and success will come effectively. You must be aware for everything to develop and grow beautifully and your patience is needed. Meditate in silence from within to construct a successful future that you are yearning for. By creating a visualized image in the mind using the power of your Inner Source, you have created your presence, and knowing what you manifested to reach the apex of your ideal life. Your vision of success and abundance will sustain every area of your life.

You become the master of your own environment, because you have the power to influence the subconscious mind to bring everything to you.

When you have an idea continue to hold that thought in the mind and terminate any negative influences. You know your positive thoughts will always be sustained by the Universal energy. The Universal energy comes from the *Universe* and the *Mind of the Universe* is the same mind as your Inner Source. When you continue feeling positive and content, you know your success is near. Even though you still have negative thought to eliminate, by remaining confident in your ideas and remaining content this will terminate any negativity to return. The negative energy will be substituted by positive influences and you will receive the benefits from your success.

A positive thought is the power of creating ideas and desires. With the positive thoughts, it triggers our body, mind and spirit act and respond to that particular idea and transmuted it into reality. It activates the mind power by using the positive thought vibrations to achieve what you want. If you believe everything you want can be achieved, then your subconscious mind will activate part of your body to make it happen and bring it to you and this is power of the mind's will.

The actual power of the mind is converting our thoughts into real reality.

By using creative visualization you have created an idea, and the keenness of the imagination is perceived in the mind's eye. You perceive in your mind's eye you are in a new profession to serve millions of people who need a particular guidance from spiritual medicine—the power of success.

You have implemented step by step suggestions and organize in details of how spiritual medicine can provide the power of success to people across the globe.

When the manuscript has been completed, it contained more than two hundred pages of text knowledge, ideas, suggestion, plans and organized information from spiritual inspiration and thought vibrations generated in the subconscious mind and translated to you. In reality, there is one mind. Mental power is spiritual power because mind and spiritual power are joined in one.

Doing well is not difficult, because you are using the power of the *Inner Source* to achieve your goals. It is in the mind reality that shapes a particular situation and instills you to make changes in your attitudes, beliefs, and habits. You always look at the bright side of life and the life you look at is transmuted to the view that you believe. If you say to yourself that you feel excellent, look excellent and be excellent. Therefore, you will. The energy brings out the "love" from within. We all share this love with each other through the power of our Inner Source. It is the power from within sustaining everything to see the real beauty and the love that surrounds us. We acknowledge the object that we look has transformed. We see the beauty through the power from within and project it to the outer world to become our own reality.

There is one thing that set us apart from other creatures on the planet Earth—the power of the mind. It helps human solve problems, overcome perplexities and difficulties and to face many catastrophes and obstacles in life. The power of the mind can help a person to build a constructive and productive life and transcend his desires into actual reality.

The mind generates two kinds of thought powers—the positive and negative. Both of these two thought powers can be transformed into physical reality. You are aware of positive thoughts are healthy vibrations, while negative thoughts are destructive energy and are unhealthy thoughts.

The concepts of positive and negative are not only used in our thought form, but it is also applied in many different fields such as mathematics, medicine and in financial institution. But, the positive and negative signs in medicine have a different representation and meaning. Positives indicate the presence in a test and negative mean absent of particular disease is found in an analysis.

Our mind is capable of generating many different forms of thoughts. It produces every idea that we need. It is like you inserting a search on a browser and many different combinations of answers will emerge for one particular solution. All answered with a solution, possible or impossible, match or unmatched to your request. It is like all these possible or impossible solutions are emerging to please you. It is as if the positive thought means *Yes I can* and the negative thought indicates *No I can't* or *I disagree*. It is for you to decide whether to accept the idea that has emerged to you.

The winning prize is to choose a positive thought and put into action. Utilize your thoughts to achieve your goals and know what particular idea is worth an extra effort to gain an achievable impulse results.

Here are the suggestions for the effective use of concentration. You must fix in your own mind that you have a definite goal and know exactly how to reach it. Then, hold that thought impulse by focusing on your intention with your eyes closed, until you can actually perceive the physical image emerging to you. Practice this exercise every day until you feel more confidence and begin to see you are actually in possession of the object!

Here is the most significant fact—the channel with **The Source**. Success will come to you when your mind, body and subliminal thought are in sync, moving you forward towards your goal of success with speed that you have never thought of or experienced before. (As you focus your perspective upon the subject, you offer a vibrational frequency either in alignment or misalignment with your Inner Source)

Do you know you can use your desktop screen to help you to filter your thought so that you can trick your subconscious mind, by making it believe that you must have that desire you are visualizing, that the object is already waiting for you to claim possession, and the subconscious mind must bring it to you and it will emerge to you all at the right time, in the right place.

You can write your own subliminal message flashing it on your desktop screen through the sixth chakra and into the subconscious mind to make an impact on you. You act upon it as soon as you received the message to achieve your dreams and desires.

Now you received the subliminal messages and acting upon it quickly, promptly, and most importantly, have the habit of reaching these decisions and quickly changing them to fit you when necessary. (You have aligned the energy with your subconscious mind.)

The subliminal message will mysteriously influence your subconscious mind with the vibrational matches between the thought you are having now and the thoughts in your subconscious mind.

You are consciously between the two vibrational frequencies, you will be in awareness of your own emotional feeling of knowing your experience and the clarity of balanced energy, success, physical fitness, and abundance and most importantly the state of joy and happiness, that is for the highest good and all concerned.

What are the obstacles to your success—Indecision, doubt, worry, and fear? The subconscious mind will not function in full capacity while these four negatives barriers are stored in your mind. The members of all evils are closely related one is emerging and the other two are at the door promptly.

Indecision is the foundation of fear. When you are unable to make a decision, you have crystallized it into doubt, and as a result these two blends together become one—fear.

The progress happens slowly and emerges without their presence being observed by you and gradually has complete control of your whole life.

Now let us put them in the spotlight and find out the cause and the cure for fears. The basic causes of fears are: poverty, ill health, the fear of being criticize, loneliness, old age and death.

Fears are constantly created in the states of mind. One's state of mind is subject to control and direction.

Fear can't emerge to you without your invitation. The opposite thoughts you are contemplating have created a negative outcome, which block you from receiving higher energy. Therefore, if you are constantly thinking of disease and illness, in that moment you will definitely find problems, which are surely related to your health and negative outcome is expected.

Furthermore, if you let many complex thoughts enter into your mind without filtering them and consider your intention you will lose your control of the mind. Fear, doubt, and worry will join your susceptible mind, which make simple things become more complex. This is how ennui set in and affects you. It is because of your vulnerable mind, which has no solid foundation or control of unstable thoughts. The uncontrolled mind is full of anger, violence, and hatred. The mind has no concrete reason to get angry. It is, as if ignited by one's fire, and then burns the whole forest and is unable to contain it. It is, as if an express train has approached before you realized, it is already on the track in front of you.

Nature has given men the power to control everything to incur the positive power of your thought. Unwanted thought leads to fear of the principal of failure by which fear may become the master.

If it is true that all thoughts are not created equal, then it is equally true that fear thought in one's mind cannot be transmuted into words of courage and financial achievement and accomplishment.

Fear and success travel in two opposite directions. If you want success and abundance, you must not let fear overpower your thought or lean towards it.

When your creative thoughts are positive, then the situation becomes, as you desired it to be, it is because you held your beliefs in place. However, when your mind is mixed with positive and negative thoughts, then the results are also indefinable. When your thoughts are trembling it is very difficult for you to achieve the desire results, because it confuses the *Universe* and your mind's reality. Even when you can obtain results, it may not be what you want entirely. However, when you change these constant thoughts to a steadier attitude, then your reality is predictable. Your lucid thought becomes the prediction in your future. It is your lucid thought and positive attitude that changes your fate.

What happens to you now will echo into your future. The future is in constant flux. This is by changing the magic power of thought vibrations in your mind. As soon as you change your thoughts, you have altered the situation you have created and then your fate changes with it. Your thoughts created that situation and is transmuted into the manifestation field and because your thoughts has been altered to override any negative creative thoughts

If you are determined to walk on the path of success, you need to acquire the power from within to hold the creation you wish to see in the outer world. You must triumph over doubtful thoughts, because you use the power of your inner source, this will bring the power needed to see victory in the physical world. When you acquire the power from within you protect yourself from harm. You must focus the power from within with a positive attitude and impulse thoughts. You follow the real power of inspiration instead of recalling from memory, you will walk on the path of abundance, health, and wealth, and the choice is yours.

Fear is an illusion and not real, but a choice. Before we make that choice, we don't know how it will turnout. The moment a choice is chosen immediately our decisions is manifested, and doubt is cleared in the mind and the ultimate results is released and known. Then, all fears become evaporated.

Your ability to influence your own feelings and emotions and experiencing the highest level of joy and happiness is within you.

Fear of poverty is a feeling of inner emptiness reflected to the external world. This thought will destroy your opportunity to achieve a goal to live a dream life. It affects your power to assess and create the life you desire. It raises low self-esteem, incapable of being interested any activity or interaction with others and lack of self-love, and ultimately these leads to uncertain future. Life becomes very difficult to manage and becomes a huge problem to your power of intention.

To remove the fear of poverty out of your life is to know and learn the knowledge from within. Knowing the knowledge will empower your awareness. Consciousness is power, the more you have it, the more energy you have to overcome all areas in your life. Energy sustains your life through the power of awareness, by making conscious connection with the dim light and to recognize the voice that guides your journey.

Fear of making decisions because lack of confidence in you will lead to indecision. Unable to accept temporary setback, laziness disrupt any chance for change and your willingness to accept the circumstance *as is* will improve life, but if you keep doubt in your mind your abilities to see success is limited and failure may occur.

Another cause of fear is fear of ill-health. It is caused by fear of old age and the fear of death. The picture printed in one's mind of what may happen if death occurs to him. These feelings are built and engraved deeply into the mind.

Finally, fear of loneliness and the fear of loss of love. It is caused by envy. The habit of being suspicious of friends and loved ones without any reasonable evidence or sufficient grounds and has no faith in no one.

The buddy of fear is worry. Worry is caused by indecision in the state of mind, which is based upon fear and can be controlled by transforming your thought or re-direct your energy to the original thought field. Once we reach a condition of openness our worry ceases.

Open your heart to accept this inner gift. It's an awareness of placing the balance of harmony with your inner peace, listens, and focuses on the center of your heart. You will immediately access a peaceful state of truthfulness.

It is time to change any limited beliefs that you have and leave it behind now and **The Source** will begin to join with you in creating the life you were intended to live. The past has no real merit. Any mistakes you made are now forgiven. You should not let fear of the past affect your potential to succeed. You live in the present. The future is only a vision. Only the present can help you to build a unique life.

You release control of events and let the *Universe* runs its course. Everything happened has a purpose and reason, but we don't know the ultimate results. The uncertainty causes many fears and worries to surface in the vulnerable mind by default. However, as soon as we pass through these processes of fears and worries, then we know there is nothing to worry about. Because, we know a clear answer that fear is only an illusion, which is created by the mental mind due to lack of faith and self-confidence and calmness in ourselves.

You are a unique individual, and your uniqueness will build the specific life you desire. To realize your potential you need to let go of your limited beliefs and release all the suppression from within and start to live in the current awareness. Only the awareness can bring your mind reality in the presence.

However, an easy way to remove fear and worry is to refine your thought and start to create fearless thoughts by using the power from within. You start by filtering your thoughts. You need to refrain from old thoughts and heal all wounds by saying to your inner self in silence: **I am sorry I love you, please forgive me. Thank you.** Keep saying this statement until you feel you are in agreement with the feelings inside that you have cleansed. You begin to adapt to this new thought pattern and eliminate worry and fear. You know and trust you can create any life you desire and you have the whole *Universe* behind you to sustain you.

You know you are responsible for everything you created and the only way to heal everything is with a simple statement saying, "**I love you.**" (Yourself)

With that said, you ask forgiveness to yourself for putting yourself in such undesirable situations and experiences. You need to be aware that you are your own Source. When you pray to God and ask for forgiveness for those unloving conditions, the outer experiences that disrupted your life and the prayer is reconnected to God and trusting God to heal you. As you begin to heal the inner self and your external world shall improve and most importantly, you need to heal the wound inside, then it will transcend the positive healing energy to the outer world.

You can embrace any fear with an open heart for peace and love. When you understand the nature of fear and the fear of being alone, doubtless of being unloved will be eliminated and released.

By practice love, peace, and forgiveness, you transform your life from hopeless to richness, and live happily and completely with an inner bliss.

You have the real power to experience your spiritual self and terminate every emotional struggle, pain, and hidden trouble. An inner peace and vision is the focal point in your life. It is the greatest gift you receive from the Universal Source.

Now your mind and thought is clear, because it is guided with a clear VISION and you know where your objective is and how to achieve it. When you know your desire the subconscious mind will make everything happen, because you are connected to intention by your desire and faith. You carry an appropriate action and you begin to see your dream being fulfilled almost magically and you continue to feel peace and harmony within. You know by the power of the *Law of Magnetic Energy* and the *Universal Mind*, anything you wish for, you will receive it.

We learn mistakes are unavoidable before any progress can take place. Any mistake you have made is good news, because it gives you opportunity to make change and one step closer to succeed. So, don't be afraid to admit your mistakes. Mistake allows you to amend your goal and future success. Understand this principal you are on your way to mastering your destiny.

You want to change your destiny, you need to make a choice, and start to eliminate all your bad habits. You need to see what you are feeling within yourself. This way of seeing will enable you to make a right decision and to live a healthy life you really want.

Your determination will help you to get rid of all your unwanted habits and recreated the life style you want and feel comfortable, peacefully and enjoyable.

You are responsible for your bad habits and they are not responsible for you. Bad habit can't control your life. You control the horizontal and the vertical. You are the master of your fate.

You want to move towards joy and happiness from despair.

You decide to make that transformation because you feel pain and your life is a total mess. You want to move towards joy and happiness from that pain and recognize change is necessary.

Pain and suffering is part of the healing transformation and a profound transformation will take place after prolong period of suffering because you have awaken. You are awakening to happiness from pain and suffering.

If you connect pain to a habit and you will certainly do everything you can to avoid that particular habit and will never occur. For example, if you install a program into your laptop. The program did not work well with your system. You will definitely remove and avoid that particular program and never use it again!

Similarly, if you install a program of your choosing into your laptop and that particular program worked abundantly fine and you start enjoying it more and more. Then, everything will become easy.

So how do you decide for everlasting change?

First off, you must decide to make that shift with the power of *Inner Source*. You must decide and know why you want to change this habit and decide to work on it until you see results. However, if your reasons are strong enough, you will change. For example, you believe that the old habit is not a benefit to your health and you determine to terminate it. Again the ultimate decision maker is you. You decide to change and know you can change. You run the show...

Now think of a habit that you want to change and feel the positive gratitude of joy and happiness you can develop, achieve, and benefit from that new transformation. While, you are experiencing positive feelings, then you continue to visualize yourself performing the task you want to reinforce in a passionate state of feeling the joy and happiness, which blessed upon you.

If you can do this exercise every morning in your waken hour, you will enforce this habit of feeling of success to reach your positive outcome. When you are actually performing it, then it will add more emotional feelings to the task you desire to transform when this occurs simply recognize it and adjust accordingly.

You can achieve your task to make changes because you have impressed upon the subconscious mind to believe that this is what you wish to receive and the subconscious mind will assist you to accomplish your desire. The subconscious mind will never miss a task unaccomplished.

Remember that you do not want to revisit again, those old habits. Then, you do not need to contemplate on them anymore and believe it will only link you with pain instead of joy and gratitude.

But you can use the pain to reinforce and focus on the new habit, instead of chasing the old unwanted habit. It is bad for your health and well-being and will hold you back.

Scientific studies show that if you can practice your habit continuously for 21 days the chance of implementing that habit, increases the success and the rates are very high. In other words, you are re-programming your subconscious mind to bring what you desire to do. And you are doing it automatically and effortlessly with pleasure and joy.

In fact, there is no specific status quo or protocol you must follow. The fact is you continue to grow, develop, or stop completely. The choice and decision is yours to make. Continue evolving your spiritual development will help you to improve every day. You are moving forward. Every door, every portal and windows of opportunity will open to you to assist your goal, and desire. You will release more energy and creativity into your life, than you could ever think of accomplishing.

Everything is achievable and possible through the power of your thoughts. The power of your thought can change, improve, or break your life. You should always focus on the positive peaceful feelings within.

Remember what you focus on will attract into your life. Same as worrying about money to pay your bills cannot help you to solve your problem. Therefore, instead of contemplating on lack of money to pay bills you should focus on your ability to handle everything that arises in front of you and your abilities to adapt to the changing world.

The lucid thought will help you to diminish any negative emotional feelings so that you can stay focused on bringing in more income.

Realize that any thought you have right now; you are inviting that essence into your manifestation field and gradually will become your own reality and experience. You realize that you can draw anything that you desire close to you for your blissful experiencing of it and you are passionate, enthusiastic about it, and because you believe in your ability to intentionally focus on those thoughts.

Most of the time you're thinking about how you can create more money to improve your financial situation. I believe you have been focusing your thoughts on how to improve or achieve a healthier body, a better relationship, and a better working environment in the work place. All of these can be done by focusing the power from within and leave the peace and the guidance of your *Source*.

I know we argue with ourselves about thinking to manifest more money, but the money has yet to come to please us. You must understand the Universal flow is an everlasting abundance and will come to you if you are steadfastly in your desire and there is no absent of abundance in your thought patterns or thinking of scarcity.

You must believe in the idea of success, abundance and prosperity is within your the vibration range, all you need to do is focus on the vibration energy until the idea of what you thought about has been felt and you will know what you are expecting is near, because of your positive awareness of emotional joy and happiness is reflected within.

You must infuse this positive attitude with emotion in your belief systems and recognize the thought energy that you apply to reinforce your feelings of wealth is gained from within. Then, you shall receive it at the appropriate time and in the designated place. Your detachment from desires allows for more time to give attention to other activities. When you detach from desire you are actually desireless. You have just created a level of trust and when you are in a high level of trusting, there is no attachment. There will be no sense of fear or worry. There's a sense of knowing, it is going to unfold perfectly, and then you realize it brings you everything. This is because you are no longer desire anymore. You are no longer wanted to control how things emerge to you. You realize you are resonating with your spirit with abundant living. As you are connected with your spirit everything comes easy to you. You are living fearlessly because you have less worries how and when things will emerge, but believe in your heart it will come to you in your own experience. You believe there is more to life than worries and how things shall occur.

When you are in alignment with *The Source*, you are actually in spiritual connection and therefore, there is no immediate need of neediness, but with eternal inner peace and calmness. Then, you realize that you should appreciate everything you already have in your life with gratitude for the infinite abundance, which the Divine Universe has provided for you.

A sense of trust and conscious connection with **The Source** becomes stronger and the emotions to help you understand the direction of your thought, and you know immediately you are moving towards or away from what you desire. There is no doubt, but understand whatever you manifested is the summoning of the power of desires and will transform into actual reality.

When a desire is inspired into an action it is later manifested into actual reality. In fact, you're actually listening and follow the intuition of your *Inner Source*. During meditation you perceive a vision in your mind's eye and you have perceived a future event happening before the actual action has taken place. Therefore, you feel strongly that the desire and action are combined through the power of Universal Source to sustain the energy to steadily flow through you. No other factor is needed in considering the accomplishment of your desire. Only the desire and you is relevant, because you know the event will happen and you have already seen it happened in a vision.

Hence, it is important that you direct your energies and aligned with your *Source*. You need to monitor your emotional feelings so that it is always in alignment with **The Source**. It is important you be vigilant in the mind because the mental mind is always searching, seeking, and coming up with many different ideas and thoughts each day that are irrelevant to the *Now*. So, it is also helpful to guard the mind, stop the unwanted thoughts to penetrate into the mind that are not relevant.

When the mind is present and things start to take shape and attract to you. Your good feelings indicate that you are in alignment with **The Source** and stay in the *Now*.

Once you understand the clarity of your emotions it is important and to know what you are hearing with your current thought. The positive energy will echo back to you and from that moment on you know the objects that you desire will be filled.

You focus on the right path to improve your life experience. You observe your thoughts flowing through you in every moment, and continue to stay in the present. You defy all vulnerable thoughts, and pay no attention to them. You center yourself and direct your thoughts to **The Source** energy.

The mind is silent, and then you realize you are free to choose the direction of your own thoughts to realize your intended goal and desire. The blissful mind reflects a joyous being from within. Your thought energy is unique, and is free to choose and activate your inner thoughts to flow towards your desire, and transcend it into the *Universal Source* and manifest everything to you.

Therefore, when you feel blissful from within is the primary step to love, health, wealth, and success, which are our Universal desires. A natural balance of body, mind, and spirit will lead to a healthy lifestyle, and along with the ability to attract abundance and prosperity. It will prevent negative thought vibrations to enter your mind. So, any time you catch yourself on a negative thought network then say to yourself **"Stop!"** and immediately re-direct your thought to the happy channel.

There are invisible forces in the Universe, which are around us and have profound influences in our lives without being seen by us. Although, these forces can't be seen by us, yet they are known to us in each moment.

For example, the electricity is an unseen force that powers everything through the power station. Thus, it is quite true to say that everything is invisible, but it is there. We are unaware of the knowledge of the Universal forces does not mean that the power is not present. The Universal force is omnipresent.

In fact, everything we felt, seen or believe is influenced by the invisible force of the *Universe*. Why we do certain things in a certain way, our thoughts are influenced by the power of the invisible force of the *Universe* that guides us. Therefore, when you are certain of what you do, you understand the laws of the Universal flow of Divine abundance, and then everything will come to you naturally and easily. This will allow you to make significant changes in your life.

The invisible force is the entrance to the power of your affection, fitness, prosperity, victory and transmutes dreams into physical veracity. We now know we have 60,000 thoughts per day and 2 per second. However, imagine that if we have one thought per day. You can imagine how powerful that thought would be to achieve your goals. No negative creativities would emerge to complicate things and make it more difficult for you to fulfill your dreams. You do this by constantly being aware of your thoughts and are able to divert thoughts to the higher energy field instead of staying in the lower energy frequency, which has no benefit to your well-being.

Do you know that you get what you feel and think about?

Everything you are offering must be a vibrational match with your feelings and emotions. Therefore, it is important for you to observe where you are in the manifest state and the process of your creation.

Your positive emotional feelings will show you where you are in the vibrational state before things manifest to you or happen in your experience, and that is because you are consciously aware of more satisfying ways to approach and express them, and intentionally you have creative power and the controlled of your own experience.

You have deliberate control of your own experience. In fact, you can always pay attention to your feelings and emotions before and after manifestation. However, it is possible that you may be unaware of manifesting in the wrong direction unless you have a desired destination in mind. Nevertheless, as soon as you are consciously aware of the direction is off the manifestation and it is never too late to re-divert your thought back to the original intention. Unless you are fully aware of each thought feeling in the manifested field, you have no way of knowing the end result.

Let's think about this in a wider view: you are aware of your surroundings and have chosen your personal preferences. Those preferences, whether you speak about it or not, enable you to make an automatic offer to the *Universe* and the *Law of Magnetic Energy* answers your request and matches them.

So consider how can you ask for more money to come to you or simply your desire to improve your life, but it did not happen?

The answer to this frequently asked question depends upon your decision and influencing facts stirring in the consciousness to create the vibrational level needed. At the moment of manifesting your desire, you are in vibrational alignment and matches to all intention in the mind. After a short period of consideration your strong desire may become less visible. Meanwhile, you have offered thoughts, which is in contrast with your original idea and your thought patterns are quite different from what you are currently asking for. Therefore, you must not change your mind or alter your thought, because what you can't see already has been manifested to you. You must be aware of this invisible power of reality and know how to push the button, and then it will ignite the fire of your manifestation. These are Universal reality, which transcend physical truth and activates your five senses that you can smell, hear, vision, touch, and taste.

That's right! When the time is right this invisible force of the *Universe* which works behind the screen will connect and will pull the string on what happened in your life.

These invisible Universal laws of nature are incorporated with the *Law of Magnetic Energy* and will attract everything you desire in your life.

These Universal laws are predictable and controllable, but you can't control how it emerges to you. When you know how to interact with the Universal Laws you will know whatever you desire will come to you.

If you paid attention to the Universal Law of manifestations, this will guide you to the right people that you desire to meet and to bring the success and prosperity in your life. It determines everything you do and don't want to manifest into your life experience.

Once you understand these Universal Laws you can start pulling the strings to create the moment according to your heart's desires, but how it's happen is up to the Universal law to bring those material into life.

Your attention to your desire is because you know the desire is real and can be transformed into physical authenticity. Although you believe the subject is real, you would like to personally experience the full effect of this, but in contrast there are also many untrue experiences you would not like to experience.

It is unimportant whether it is real or not is because you want to experience the truth of it in your manifestation experience. You are reminded that anything you focus on long enough will be activated and become reality. That is the invisible Universal laws of creation associate with the **Law of Magnetic Energy** to connect your dreams into actual reality. No exception!

Your success will be immediately uplifted at that moment you understand and begin to utilize your own emotional feelings to connect with your idea and the **Laws of Magnetic Energy**.

Through the continual exposure to your own power and the awareness of emotional feelings, you are consistently focusing on desires the whole day, and activating a vibration within you. Therefore, you are attracting your own reality. Your intentional thought that you focus upon becomes actuality.

In this material and fast-pace world, it is unlikely you have conscious awareness of every thought. In fact, it is almost impossible to sort and process all thoughts that gain entry into our mind. Luckily, you don't need to sort or process them because of the **Law of Magnetic Energy** will sort them for you. It is because everything is light (consciousness) and vibrates with energy. Your consciousness is your own consider experiences and preferences and is being created from that personal perception. You are asking the Universal Mind from the consciousness and the vibrational energy connected to the Source in knowing what you are manifesting through your thoughts.

Your Inner Source receives the request and is aware of your desires, and transforms those whole ideas into desires, which you have manifested. In other words, your thought and desire are in alignment to your *Source* and therefore, you immediately receive the benefit of this result. Because, it happens so quickly, your physical mind may not be aware of the immediate results, due to the fact it takes a while to eliminate all mixed feelings. Gradually, you and the subconscious mind are constantly connected, which brings about the vibrational matches to your desire and becomes physical equivalent.

For example, sorting out all your mail, you realize you have lot of bills that needs to be paid. However, you realize you do not have sufficient money to pay all your bills. A desire for more money is manifested and your Inner Source immediately focuses on and works out a solution for you. But, unconsciously you are still focusing on the problem of paying your bills. You are not in alignment with your *Inner Knowing* that brings your needs.

You have not connected with your desire and the negative feelings indicate your misalignment with **The Source**. Unless you correct the negative thought vibrations there will be a vibrational difference between your desire and you're actual thought energy. You must believe in your practical preference that you have more than enough money to pay bills and plenty left over to spend. In other words, you must realize your desired experience must be aligned before they will become an actual experience. It is important to monitor your emotional and vibrational feelings and it helps you to understand and recognize the relationship between the energy of your desire and you. Then, your desire can be manifested and transform into a realistic experience. One thought joined with one mind to manifest your desire into actuality. You know where your current situations are and where you want to be is the emotional feelings you receive. Your current relationship between how much money you have in your financial situation and the amount of cash you would like to receive in your bank account is the basis of the emotional feelings that you received. In your state of mind you desire the amount of money you would like to have in your bank account, but your consciousness must be met with the right action.

The ultimate action is the lucidity of thought and the activation of your desires, so that you are not shuffling from thought to thought to eliminate clutter in your mind, but to strengthen your beliefs in your desire.

Wish and yearning for a desire is different from being ready to accept it. Nobody is ever prepared to accept anything unless he truly believes that he can obtain it. The mind must be in the state of believing and not just hoping and wishing for something. A Closed mind never inspires courage, faith or the power to believe. Your old beliefs can always be adjusted, modified, and changed.

When you change your old beliefs and implement new ideas to your current conscious state of mind and it will impress your subconscious mind and to agree to make changes meeting your needs and transmuting your desire into a goal of success.

For example:

I wish to see my book selling successfully and abundantly on publishamerica.com.

Now compare to this desire:

I no longer feel stressed when I learn that my book is selling successfully and abundantly on publishamerica.com now.

The second statement is in vibrational match to my thought intention and desire. So, I follow the second statement to manifest my desire, because of the clarity of thought; I know I am going to get my desired results. The clarity of my thought vibration aligned with my *Inner Knowing* and finds alignment with the idea of my intention, which brings vibrational harmony with the Universal Mind. Eventually, it will transmute my desire into actuality. Love, tranquility, and patience are the essence in the manifestation to receive your desire and success. I follow my feelings, and let go of control and resistance. Consequently, I believe in my strong faith and inspire encouragement and to obtain what I truly desire.

The above example shows that the lucidity of thought, faith, and belief with your desires brings your power from within and combines with your knowledge of self and **The Source** to bring into alignment the desire results.

You must experience your own creation and find your own desired results.

In a materialistic world, nothing is free. If you want to take spiritual lessons or join a spiritual retreat then you must pay a price to gain that experience. Wealth and success also has price to pay before we can reach triumph. The price to achieve what you desire is in the power of your vibrational thoughts or the power of mind.

Whatever you desire to do, to have or to be you must give your full attention and energy to it.

For example:

If you want to become a lawyer, you must go to law school and obtain a law degree. However, there is a price to pay. You devote 4 years of making every effort and dedication to obtain this degree. You are an experience lawyer now after long years of practicing law. In fact, it is your subconscious mind that automatically guides you to achieve the **Hall of Fame** in your professional field. The price you paid is during the time of your study and your determination to obtain a law degree. Your faith leads you to do what you do and the subconscious mind helps you to fulfill your desired results. However, if you don't pay attention to devoting time, energy and have belief in what you do, then you will never thrive, and have no results.

Another example:

You desire to buy a notebook, but you do not want to lock in all your cash. However, an option opens to you. You can pay by monthly installment. But, you are unwilling to sign a 3 years lease contract with Dell financing. Ok, you don't want to pay cash and you don't want to pay interest so at the end what do you get. You probably will know the end results.

The above example shows that you want to obtain something and you must be willing to pay a price or else you will have nothing in the end.

You endorse your action with faith by deliberately choosing vibrational thoughts and consciously pay attention to details and signals around you; your vigilance and emotional feelings have strengthened the power of attraction and you have successfully utilized your power of success to achieve anything you desire and deserve.

Faith comes by understanding the thought of the mind and applying it diligently in all your endeavors.

For examples:

Scientists have faith and trust in their endeavors to achieve their goals, and someday this will lead to understanding more about the mystery of the Unknown Universe. Farmers have faith that the seeds planted in the ground will result in a good harvest.

So, before you can reach a specific goal and desire, you must have faith that you will reach it. You can cast positive thoughts, and follow your heart's direction. The vibration will have a great deal of influenced on the power of your desires and thoughts. When you focus your thoughts long enough, you consciously create and direct everything. It awakens this wonderful inner power of the subconscious mind where we integrate ideas and desires to be shared with the world. When you join with your good feelings in every area of your life this will indicate the chances of receiving your desire is near, and the thought vibration is powerful enough for manifestation to occur. Your determination, persistence, and the integration of the mind's reality will bring every success in your life.

When you understand the power is from the Inner Source, you have acquainted yourself with the higher level of knowledge needed to succeed and see life differently. You understand things that others don't and achieve everything with ease.

Remember, your thoughts equal vibration and it will be answered by the Law of Magnetic Energy.

For example:

You have written a book and believe it will become a great book someday. You send your manuscript to various publishers, but no results. However, you determine to publish your book and start focusing on the good feelings within your thoughts. You begin to work on the inner power of your thoughts, and you perceive a vision of your book being manifested with inner bliss, and realize you have creative control over that desire. Furthermore, you continue to be focused on the results of your positive thoughts as they are unfolding. Your willpower and persistence will guide you towards the success you deserve. You do not have any doubts in your mind that your entire dream will become a dream reality.

Another example:

You wish to manifest and gain the wealth that you deserve from the *Universe*. You begin to visualize wealth coming your way because of being attentive and keeping faith in your desire. However, after holding your thought for a period of time, you are slightly off-course, and started to add your desire with mixed positive and negative thoughts. When your thoughts are trembling it is very difficult for you to achieve the desire results, because it confuses the *Universe* and your mind's reality.

You do not hold that thought long enough to guide yourself steadily towards your goals. You are still focusing on lack and forget your original desire and intention. You have shifted this field from your higher energy thought vibration to a lower frequency thought. Since you have detour your energy and echoes a different intention, therefore, you can't expect to see result.

(For example, two race cars are racing each other on the racing tracks. The red sports car is moving at a speed of 5 hundred mph, while the blue sports car is only moving at 3 hundred mph. It is impossible these two cars will meet each other unless the red car slows down, then the blue car will have a chance to meet the red car. The speed of the red sports car is too high for the blue car to realize. The red sports car becomes invisible to the blue sports car because of it trailing behind.)

If you constantly changed your thought how do you expect the desire to manifest to you? You keep adding new energy to your thought and energy will fluctuate because you are constantly adding new ideas that don't match with the original thought. It is not the same vibrational match and does not generate the same energy.

The power of thought is energy and energy is in constant state of motion. Your new idea transcends into the *Universe*, but can't match with the other, because they are in two different thought fields. The two thoughts are not synchronized or in harmony. Then, what will happen? They echo back to you with a different result than expected. Nothing will manifest. In order to manifest your desire all your vibrational thoughts must be attuned to your ideas to receive effective results.

You must treat your goals and desires that have materialized with gratitude and acceptance that this *Universe* has brought this to you.

Most successful people of the past and in this modern age have one thing in common, they are able to cancel all negative suggestions, and discourage influences from friends or relatives, and follow their own intuitions as intended until they succeed. Persistence becomes an important factor for their successes.

There are many aspects to success and the gaining of materials riches are inclusive to creating one's desire in this material world. Success will never end in one phase even when that stage is completed. It is an expedition; continued exploration, but not a final destination. Wealth is an expression of joy and happiness that leads to success, opportunity, and gratification. However, health and love must be included in your abundant life.

It is not difficult to accumulate wealth into a desired fulfilled life; if we know how to live in serenity with nature we create a conscious connection between that desire, and the power to manifest those aspirations to become reality.

Hidden deep within, you have an unknown place of infinite power. Deep down inside you can find love, peace, joy, and happiness forever expanding freedom filled with the Divine power of inexhaustible higher energy. You consciously enter into this Divine place within where your life can be made in that moment.

It is the true nature of success that this innate power implanted within, where you can acquire knowledge, gain vision, and obtain productivity, and to renew your life. You can eliminate fear, worry, stress, and negative beliefs and bad habits to recognize this infinite power of success is far beyond your imagination. All you have to do is unleash it.

When you tap into the hallow place of the unknown and it is the fertile grounds where you can manifest everything you want. When you enter into this space between hallows and the silence you will feel tranquil and peaceful. It is the place full of fertile resource and imagination can come true. Dreamer can create visions of veracity and transform them into physical form. In the hallow places you can convey your concern to the Source and search for the eternal wisdom from the mysteries of the unknown. Within the unknown you can manifest anything you desire with least effort, and at anytime with no restriction.

When you are in the place of the unknown it opens a whole range of possibilities and are not limited to one path, but many opportunities are receptive to you. You are conscious of yourself and recognize both as being manifested in the crystal world and the invisible world. Hence, consciousness lays at **The Sources** in life's achievements.

The purpose of giving and receiving is to keep the *Universe* flow of abundance continuing and circulating into the cosmic and for everyone to benefit. Money falls into this category of circulation and a token of exchange for goods and services.

Hence, it fits into the Divine purpose of giving and receiving. Money represents a movement of current awareness and is constantly meant to flow steady. Money is not meant to be kept in the bank, but you must allow it to run freely, so that its energy will flow back to you and others around you.

The idea of giving generously will benefit you. It is as if you tell the Universe that sharing wealth brings more joys and happiness and the realization of abundance is coming from the Divine Universe. You desire to build that joyful relationship between the **DIVINE UNIVERSE** and you. Because you understand this therefore, you return the wealth back to the community to show your gratitude.

When you donate money to charity there is no relationship, but your intention is to give a free gift to benefit others. However, it is different than hospitality because you can relate to it with mutual benefit; a return of kindness to someone forms a bond of connection.

It is a healthy habit; it can extend life when one feels that sense of inner urge to do and bring joys and peace to others.

For example:

If friends bestow blessings to you for all good things and health in your life, you will always give blessings back to them silently.

For example:

Giving and sharing the energy with each other will sustain and change life. It is not only one-person effort of transcending the energy to the other. It is when one gives his energy to another that this exchange create a positive bond both in the mind and the feelings that connect with relationship of our abilities to share this energy of love. If we all doing this it will keep the energy alive to flow infinitely and return back, and translate into everyone own realty.

Conversely, it is a benefit to send blessings to nature and this will return good things to you in mysterious ways. Therefore, a good bond must remain.

Your act of compassion will bestow you with many blessings from **The Source** someday, because you chose the right action that brings joy and bliss to those around you and that idea eventually becomes part of you. Every cause always comes with an effect. The effect is the cause of the reaction to the force of energy and returns to you equally.

Every day we perform many activities either knowingly or unknowingly in a subtle way, which has a great influence on what life brings to us. Our lives will change moment by moment and is influenced by the power of thought.

Your decision is based on the thought you have in the mind and influenced mentally from past experience. The decision that you make has consequences that are either constructive or destructive.

Therefore, you're unbroken thought and positive action will transform complexity and perplexity into triumph. It is important that before you make a decision ask yourself what are the consequences of my choice? Indeed, there is only one decision, the precise choice, which brings joy, happiness, and success to you and all concerned.

You pay attention to how you feel the moment the decision is made. You watch your bodily gestures and reaction. If you respond comfortably and feeling good, then the choice you made is appropriate for you. The future of your life is generated by your decision for a good assessment, and a steadfast decision in the present and what happens to you now will echo into your future.

When you let go of control of everything many amazing things will emerge to you effortlessly. You could find ways to be satisfied by the use of non-resistance in your life. Whatever turmoil and disharmony has happened in your life, you are operating against the basic attitude of non-resistance, and consequently it leads to dissatisfaction, anger, and frustration. Do not compromise your thinking by focusing on despair in order to separate the pros from the cons. Chances are it may take a while for a solution to emerge, but stay flexible and use your common sense and vigilance to be responsive to the signals that guide you to the solution. Suddenly, you have identified the disorder and are due to bad decisions and subsequently you have created the undesired experience of turmoil.

If you recognize everything happen is a result of that choice then you must be clear in your mind how to make the changes needed to reflect the results you expect.

Then, you should look for the right response to eliminate the despair in each situation. You must pay attention to change the negative thoughts and feelings to eliminate the chaos and take time to look inside to recognize how unnatural it is.

To fix this chaos effectively and successfully you need cling to all positive thoughts and trust in the process to produce change and incur control of events in your life. Once your life starts improving, then the next step is to ask the *Universe* to bring more joys and comforts into your life. You begin to release the level of resistance by non-resistance. So, if you are not trying to resist your desire, you are moving towards the Universal Source. You feel your desire will achieve whether it is a material object or a relationship, a condition and the standard of success is actually the amount of joy you feel.

There is always a solution for everything and similarly there is always a way to fulfillment. There is no dead end or piles of dead stone if you let nature take its course or simply be. You accept thing as they are and believe everything happen for a reason and everything happen for the best, even if the condition didn't occur there is nothing really missing, but you have peace within. It is the simplest way of manifesting desire naturally, automatically, and with ease and the result is always amazing, and manifestation of that thought becomes realized. Steadfastly, you put in very little effort, but accomplish more. Finally, you don't need to do anything, but actively engage in life.

When you connect with the *Inner Source* and you fire up your desires, and transmute the conscious action into the power of success.

221

Conscious action is how you feel inside yourself and how you will act to the external world.

The thought is silent and motionless until it is ignited into action by your desires. When you transcend your conscious thought into the *Universe*, and aware there is a choice, then you have invited the invisible power of the Universe to work for you. Therefore, when you focus on your thoughts, you have the power to change.

This invisible intelligence was given to you the moment you were born. With this infinite power you can improve the quality of your life, and the awareness of your thoughts and the environment around you. You attract more love, abundance, health, and success into your life, and create a desirable life in the most possible ways.

However, the *Universe* responds best when you are detached from your desire. You no longer feel stress and are unconcerned about getting it or not. In other words, you are not desperate or obsessed. You understand the power of detachment and are able to maintain the unshakable calmness while being committed to your goal with a strong passion.

Detachment eliminates paying attention to the outcome, but you still intend to have it. Your intention is focused on the future and the attention is manifested in the present. When the quality of the intention and your imagination meet with each other, it mirrors your goals and desires in the physical world. Then, all your dreams and desires will transform and manifest into material reality.

We all have visions that we wish to fulfill the meaning of life. In fact, we also have a unique gift from the *Universe* that enables us to contribute our special talent to help each other. Because of everyone's intention is unique and your uniqueness has urged you to inquire silently within and to seek the Universal plans for you.

The plan of the *Universal Mind* is for you to experience life, and be aware of your Higher *Consciousness Self* and consciously connected with **The Source** to receive the visions of your dreams and ultimately reach

each of your goals. You know you are part of creation and the bridge between you and the *Universe* is self love. Therefore, you need the *Universe* to sustain you in every aspects of your life to achieve the success you deserve. When you are master of your purpose, you have the whole *Universe* to aid you. You realize your life is much easier than you thought. It is because you have let go of details and hand it over to the *Universe*.

Therefore, in every corner of your mind the invisible force comes to endorse and sustain you and feel its strength and vibration is above, below, around, behind, and within you.

Your awareness of life's purpose manifests miracles in every venture and brings along with it peace and success. It is because you have provided ample service to other to bring success to them. You believe by helping others to succeed, you will receive the abundance you desire. You have more energy and ability than before to have many great ideas come to you effortlessly. You are more motivated and passionate about what you inspire to do. You have drawn to you everything that gives full expression of joy and being a part of creation. All because you have seen a dream and vision of what you can create on this planet Earth.

Similarly many successful inventions continue to succeed, because the inventor knows his purpose is inspired. Yet, many successful and powerful people are not seeking for more ways to obtain monetary gain, but to provide ways and the means to help others because they realize their genuine purpose. In fact, if everyone is doing what has inspired them to do is a *Divine* purpose and believes there is no scarcity, and then abundance of opportunities will open to them. Indeed, we have only consumed 4 percent of the whole Universe resources, and therefore it has plenty for everyone to share in this huge pie without competition. What the Universe has done for others, **The Source** can do for you!

So for you to live abundantly you need to serve as many people as possible. In return, through you it will dissolve all obstacles to reach the highest good and let the Universal flow uninterrupted and to increase power of success and to become prosperous.

Money is not the reason why you provide your service to others. It is a reward to you for your knowledge, or service and the job that you enjoy doing. It is a way of showing gratitude for a job well done.

Success does not mean following what other tells you to do, but by exploring your inner landscape, where no one else has gone before, like The Voyager. You will be the pioneer and create your own image of success.

Divine imagination inspires the right actions and establishes higher respect and reputation, that leads to unexpected opportunities presenting them; the moment it was built and the power of faith and belief, endless energy has guided you to reach the pinnacle of the pyramid. You have trained others on how to use their own mind powers to create visions of a successful path and to manifest their dreams and desire.

Every success there is a Divine plan; a vision of what you perceive inside is the result of you visualizing what you perceive in the physical world. Your current reality is a reflection of what is occurring in the mind.

The cosmos operates according to a set of Universal Laws and you need to be aware of this power, if you want to succeed in your effort to create and manifest your own reality.

How often do you hear someone say that they are having a run of either good or bad luck? We realize that there are external factors that are at work in our daily lives. Some call this Lady Luck, Fate, Karma, or even a simply unknown factor. No matter what we may call it, we can't get away from the fact that the unknown factors or good luck is one of the most important ingredients in a person life. However, do you need good luck to draw success to your endeavors? Is good luck a Divine scheme or simply a coincidence? What is good luck?

In fact, good luck is an event that embraces with positive vibrations to work for us. This is especially true when circumstances are random and can't be predicted or controlled by you. You may call it a coincidence, but you know better, don't you! There is indescribable quality of power to those who possess this kind of "***good luck***." They are confident mainly because they recognize that everything works out well for them. They believe life does not always come by battling and all things are made of energy, there is unbounded amount of energy in the *Universe* that everyone can assess and is waiting for you to bring it into your life.

You have the power to improve good health, financial security, and also a gift of inner guidance and protection at your command to help you enjoy all the good things that this earthly life has to offer. Absolutely! No one would deny or refuse to accept this unbelievable inner source of energy. All you need to do is activate the spiritual power within and accept it in the Now.

If you feel unfortunate because of lost of possessions you once owned. You should cancel that thought now. When you truly own something, you can never lose it entirely. Material possession is only *temporary*. When it comes, it pleases you, when it leaves you it may be a bad thing. Accept and enjoy it while it is in your acquisition, but spend less time holding on because it will evaporate. Worry and stress will never compensate for your lost, so let the *Universe* do its own thing to compensate you naturally.

By dismissing all negative thoughts you no longer feel stress in the mind and are clear to actively connect to **The Source**. You are clearing all this clutter and your mind becomes lucid. If you have many desires, you must choose to activate only one thought at a time and ask the *Universe* to manifest a vision for you. You monitor and stabilize your emotions to match with your mental focus.

Again, is good luck a Divine plan or coincidence? When you are directing your thought power to the invisible Universe to eliminate any unwanted circumstance in your favor and knowing the *Universe* responds to your request. Since the *Universe* is able to create unity and harmony for your life, you will begin to see the effects of this power to make changes and move towards success and it is necessary to be thankful for what you do have.

This begins by instill faith and belief in this invisible power that you can assess and the Universe will respond according to your desire and wish. If you seem to lack funds, you must remain thankful and grateful for what you have, and let the *Universe* knows that you trust that more riches is coming to you shortly.

Your thought power added to the subconscious mind and filling it with positive energy created in the mental consciousness will give the impressions to the *Universe* that you have finished your creation and it will reinforce a wonderful change in your life.

Now you know the power for good luck is connected to **The Source** within and apply the Universal Laws to help you to achieve what you desire and see the abundance that is freely given to you. Everything that you have is the result of your thoughts and desires. You must be convinced of what you already have created within otherwise you can't receive from the physical world.

The truth is what you envision are your own thoughts manifesting inward. Everything does happen for a reason and **The Source** guides and allows these events to happen. You must create an inner conviction that the Laws work and then you become a magnet of positive energy and everything you desire comes to you.

Those people who are aware of the Universal's abundance purposefully direct their thought energy to uplift their lives and for that reasons they are connected to the results from within. They don't worry about people around them and they don't doubt themselves. They know this can be destructive and refrain from doing so.

Instead of arguing with people, successful people will identify the cause and will allow them to see clearly the current situation. They will determine whether the desire is worth acknowledging.

Successful people are engaging and have a different way of doing thing from ordinary people. They don't just say, "*I'll try it*" but rather **"yes, I can."** They have a very affirmative attitude and never doubt about their abilities. They are not afraid to say "no." They believe in themselves and follow their visions to completion. They believe in faith and act on it quickly. Their determinations and enthusiasm is why success emerges to them so quickly and effortlessly.

If you want to succeed, you shouldn't let your thought be dominated by your emotions and feelings of doubt. The path that you are on is guided by your impulsive thoughts and then you follow this.

The quality and the condition of your thoughts relate to your emotions and feelings are leaning towards positive energy. Because, whatever you are thinking now will reflect what your future will be.

Thoughts have spirit. Every emotional thought will add extra power to your consistent thoughts. So, what are you thinking? What is in your mind now? If you are thinking optimistic thoughts, then your energy is currently aligned with *The Source*. Your positive emotion is a clear indication of your alignment with *The Source* energy. When you include enthusiasm into your thought, you are actually raising the energy and transferring this towards your desire. When you feel good about your original thought you have actually reactivated and empowered its energy to flow through the Universe, and someday return to you with a validated result.

For example:

You focus on an idea of buying a new home and it does make you feel good. You have communicated this thought to your inner being regarding this idea. Then, you begin to create a visualized image adding your energy to influence the power of your thought to activate your ideas, which will cause your energy to increase each time you perceive this new home. As the thought vibration expands to build momentum and this energy surrounding you will flow to increase the influence of your thought energy towards this new home, a feeling of calmness and peace, because you are near to getting this new home. The thought vibrations continue to gain strength and your emotion responds to your thoughts and begins to attract similar energy to clarify your thoughts. As the thought gains momentum, you begin to feel this emotional thought is matching the energy of your Source.

The more positive energy adds momentum and increases your

ability to attract your dream home and will become a reality, because of the *Law of Magnetic Energy* to bring this to you.

However, you need to be vigilant with your thoughts, which may lean toward negative thought field. You must continue to observe and deliberately choose your direction and this thought directs the affects of your own attraction. Then, you will continuously to be on course and navigate towards the vibrational state of feeling good to bring your desire closer to you. You must be aware of any negative thoughts that will weaken the aptitude to achieve your goal. Your thought vibration is now aligned with your desire and **The Source**, positive energy is flowing towards you without resistant. Since there is no resistance you have allowed your desire to flow back to you and transmute your thought vibrations into physical veracity.

When your mind, body, and spirit are in alignment with **The Source,** you are immediately aware of your request emerging to you. You always have access to the Universal supply of unlimited abundance, and any desire you fancy without limitation and you hold absolute power of controlling your desire.

Your own emotional thoughts can affect your desire to succeed. You should only select emotional thoughts that give you the abilities to move towards a higher energy thought field to fulfill the desires of your dream.

Your determination, persistent and faith are the starting points to manifesting your heart's desire. When you match these requirements to achieve your desire, the windows of opportunity will open to you and everything will come to you in peace. As long as you are consciously aligned with **The Source**, the item you are asking for will flow into your experience.

You consciously connect your Inner Self with **The Source**, and follow your bliss and in that moment your well-being is awaken to everything. Any desire you want to achieve will become possible, but only with peace of mind. When you do, your inner world will transform everything you desire into a physical equivalent.

When you consciously connect with **The Source** about your dream and desire and you must eliminate all fears, worries and doubts in the mind, be receptive to your open-mindedness and your conscious thoughts. As, you continue to deepen the peace of the mind from within to navigate your life. Without attachment this allows the *Universe* to connect with your subconscious mind and creates something that you seek. This process will take care of itself automatically and effectively.

Your conscious mind is constantly seeking and searching for different things from time to time. It will never stay in one place, but constantly bring in new thoughts without you being aware of them. When the mind is finally calm and still, now you are fully embedded in the **Now** and this is when you take control of the mind and directs your thought to align with **The Source** and that's the ability to obtain your desire. This can be attained by inner meditation and the stillness of the mind to receive inner peace and calmness.

I understand we want to get things quickly, but everything happens in the *Universe*, there is a Divine time line and you will receive it when the time has matured.

In fact, there are many things manifested to you every day, you may not realize them. You have many wonderful things manifesting to you and the extra attentions you give to this small tiny miracle and the more of those beautiful things will attract to you.

However, you must be in the moment to realize and enjoy them. If you are in the middle of savoring a wonderful soup and you start thinking of other things at the same time. Then, you have missed the opportunity of joining with that moment to enjoy the energy generate by the soup, which enhances your body's connection to this experience. Remember you must appreciate small things that come to you in the now and there is no need to be concerned about other things. Your desires must be in the now for you to create them, and then you know you are on the right path. All other substances will emerge to you automatically, because you are fulfilled in the *Now*.

Everyone wants everything immediately and when it does not happen we start second guessing it all. The moment you second guess it you have added a counter thought to your original thought. The counter thoughts are negative energies that are different from your original thoughts.

The moment that you are derailed, you have disrupted your creative path. It is no longer coming to you. So you need to learn to channel your thoughts on what you really want and empower your thoughts with the creative field to keep you on the path of success.

You need to trust this inner ability and to join with the *Universal Source* to add energy to your request and just let go. Then, you let the *Universe* delivery to you in its own time, knowing and believing in your own creation and once you have put the order in it is coming. The more relax you are the faster it will come to you. ***Do not over think about this.*** You must continue to believe you are in the flow to receive the abundance that is actually coming to you. Then, you begin to understand you need to appreciate them and then they will emerge. Yes, you deserve abundance and acquisitions from the Universal Source. You want a big trunk of money emerge to you, only when you learn to appreciate a small miracle and be grateful for its forth coming, then greater opportunity will come to you effortlessly and effectively.

In focusing your mind on positive attitudes will deepen and influence the decision in your mind and affirm the ideas and performing the creative visualization to follow through to your desires. So in order to get what you want you must reprogram your mind to believe you already have the things you want and the subconscious mind brings this to you.

Your subconscious mind responds faster because of the strength of your wants, but if your thoughts and emotions are mixed, these negative emotions enter automatically to interfere with your desires. However, the positive emotions have the power to change and directed your thought impulses that add to making real change in the mind. This will allow your mind to be receptive to the power of the invisible source influencing your emotional thoughts to stay on course.

These emotions and feelings in the mind constitute an important element in your thought form held in the collective mind and transferring this actual activity to reality and creating its existence.

You intentionally create this formless substance associated with your thoughts and eventually it will become your actual truth. Therefore, you should concentrate your energy on the subject of what you desire, banish any negative thoughts, and embrace your mental mind with affirmations of success. In other words, you send a *message of success* to your subconscious mind and transmute the quality of your thought; your action will then be strong and decisive. While, you face difficulties you believe the subconscious mind will support you with higher energy, greater strength and better decision making, because you deliberately train you mental mind to align with who you are, and your external world will also fall into alignment with your physical being and will show itself to you in all areas of your life experience.

The most common uses of creative positive emotions are desire, intention, faith, action, and reality.

In addition, the negative emotions are fear, envy, hatred, revenge, greed, and anger.

You must be aware positive and negative emotions can't tolerate each other. You must determine which one you want to set as your "*default.*"

We can overcome life's complexities and confusions through the power of our thoughts and a strong belief in this innate power to bring influential experiences to our lives. It means our problems must be boldly met to conquer this thought of confusions. It is advised that you should hold positive and reflective thoughts and you are responsible for your own action. Therefore, it is your responsibility to make sure these positive thought holds a strong dominate power in your mind. It is important that you fill your conscious mind with creative thoughts to gain love, health, wealth, success, peace, and happiness. If you surrender all your problems to the subconscious mind and then the conscious mind will be liberated from worry, fear, and stress. Simple discipline of mental thought in the conscious mind is necessary to facilitate an inner change that has taken place. The power to overcome complexity in life is the use of thought energy, because it helps us to develop a steadfast mind. With a steadfast mind, there is no difficulty and confusion in our life's experience. We can resolve anything in our life experience with faith in the ability of our mind and joining with this innate power found within to help us through successfully and effortlessly.

We talk to God like he is our best friend with love and have the faith in *His* love for us; because God is love and *He* love us. Prayer is simply a conversation with God, expressing your feelings and emotions to *Him*. Hence, it is a way of communication to our Creator and the *Mind of God*. Prayer has a direction. Your prayer is directed and addressed to God and you acknowledge *His* presence and existence and created a mutual trust in the relationship. God response also has a direction and you will not be left to adrift or wander. Your prayer will be answered if you trust *Him*, love *Him*, and remain with *Him*.

There are two levels of prayer that reach God. The physical level is transmuting word of prayer through the mental mind to the consciousness. Then, in the spiritual level, the subconscious mind will convert the words into the rate of vibration to transcend it into the *Universe* so that **The Source** can understand you. Subsequently, the message will return with an answer in the form needed for you and God will guide you in that plan, which is designed for you.

God is the sources of all powers; you can't attain this power, knowledge, or wisdom without consciously aligning with God. You attain your real wisdom by meditating on the *Inner Source*, and you gain the truth and faith about yourself. When you know the truth you echo these inner powers, wisdoms and knowledge and know where you're coming from. With this power in store you will do the right thing at the appropriate time and emerge at the right place. Others will admire your abilities and trust you to make the right decision and lead them.

Because, you always know your direction your accurate decision is obtained and inspired from within. Hence, you believe that nothing can be misguided because of your unity with **The Source**. The attainment of this power is always from **The Source**. **The Source** is the power of all powers.

The power to great success in life is within this latent ability of the subconscious mind and waiting for you to use its great wisdom. Our wisdom is limited, unless we align our mind with knowledge greater than us, and draw from it inspiration. Real wisdom knows the right thing to do at the right time and in the right place without hesitation and this truth is received only from God. The real wisdom aids you to perceive the spiritual insight and inspiration because of the unity with **The Source**, and this allow you to do the right thing and implementing a steadfast decision or assessment to take the appropriate courses of action. You emerge in the right place and your unwavering faith in God and decision to be in the appropriate place has created joy in you and God. Faith is you can depend upon God in giving you the ultimate success and victory. To obtain this *Inner Wisdom* it requests no sacrifice or hard work and perhaps there is no special requirement for advanced educational background. Everyone can do this at their own disposal with little effort, but you must acknowledge it. Successfully people understand using their own power of imagination to meet their desires. They realize to be successful one must use inspiration from within and imagination, vision in their planning and the right course of action to succeed.

However, if you desire to enter into any professional field, then you **must** obtain a degree(s), to deepen your knowledge, a definite purpose and a burning desire and a commitment until the end. Remember, your success is partially due to the expression of God's love, but not completed. You need to keep your faith and express your love to God; because God is perfect and only by uniting with God you become one with *Him* and success will follow.

You must catch the spirit of great pioneers of the past whose dreams have given civilization the importance of utilizing their strength and talent to create success and opportunity, to see that we can follow in their footsteps to create the world we want to see.

These great people have put their talents into great inventions; practical use of thoughts to convert this power into building such ideas, as electricity, aircrafts, cars and different forms of convenience that make life easier and comfortable.

If you have a dream and you believe in it, go for and do it! Put your dream into action and you will never fail. For those who do not try will never know that every failure brings the seed of ultimate success. Success is in your dream, but failures will not defeat you if you don't doubt yourself. A real dreamer will never quit his dream until he transforms it into physical equivalent. Like the Wright brothers dreamed of an engine to fly into the sky.

Because of their enthusiasm it has shown that others can follow their dreams and explore new ideas of venturing into the black outer space to reach the moon and mars, because of their great spirit of inventions and they dreamed powerfully.

You live in an unlimited Divine abundance. Your spiritual heart holds the key for that richness, which is for you to explore that burning idea, ambition and to create an experience that comes your way to help you to set your goals until some day you turn your dream into reality. Remember great successes come with a price and no one succeeds without paying a cost.

The reality is you will never lose, when you try and success is amazing.

Being born with a generic disease and gone through many years of misfortune and finally he is able to preprogram his mind and tap into the innate power to help himself resolve life and ultimately he takes control of his life by manifesting it, exactly as he wishes.

"*Yatel*" was born with a genetic disease with no known cure and nobody in his family has this disease. Although he was brought up with a good background, but at his younger age he didn't understand God had a purpose for him. He was angry with the nature of his disease and that has inhabited his life. He was a loner and did not have many friends. Nobody wanted to get to know him or become a friend. As age goes on in his mind he knew he is not just "*Yatel*" and he could do better.

Opportunity and luck did not become his way. But in his mind he never gave up on what his purposes was.

After fifty years of struggling in life, finally a profound opportunity had come and has radically transformed his life into a new image. He has encountered the power of the Divine Light in him. He recognizes now that he has a Divine purpose. A voice from above has inspired him to write this book and use his misfortune to help others.

Five years ago guided by inspiration, he began to write his first book *"**THE AWARENESS OF MAGNETIC ENERGY**.*" His book has gotten published and he has never felt sorry for his misfortunate again. Now he believes strongly that there is no such thing as misfortune, or bad luck, but with the Divine purpose, he experiences life on Earth in a new light. We all create our own reality and everything occurred because of what you thought in your mind and we live in the present to continue experiencing them in the future. No one will have misfortune until adversity has been accepted as reality.

"Yatel" is aware of his Infinite self and discovers what it takes to live life to the fullness. He no longer feels whom he once was and is connected to the whole, because he understands the unity with the Divine and has transformed himself and continues living in the moment, which brings him back where the opportunity of this relationship exists. He realizes it is the moment where real transformations take place and all related circumstances.

He loves and admires each moment that brings him success and the connection to love and believes whatever defeated him in life was only a lesson to learn and experience. It is a way to convey a peaceful solution to feel better and improve his life. The state of mind must inspire belief, but not just hopes and wishes. Keeping an open mind is the power of belief. Closed minds do not inspire faith and trust.

Oftentimes, it is in the silent conversation that you permit the negative emotions and feelings to emerge and this is why you feel despaired and upset. Talking to yourself with positive thoughts will allow you to improve your life and act on it. Although negative thoughts can be negated this will allow positive thoughts to return and are used to benefit your life.

Nonetheless, it is impossible that you can shut down all negative feelings and emotions, but be aware of their existences; to acknowledge them is the best effort. It is from there you will discover that everything is good. You learn nothing bad can happen unless you have allowed it to happen. When you can relax and observe what is in your circumstances that you don't like, you can cancel the situations easily and quickly. You know better what kind of life you desire and **who you should be**, and keep your life in order. You have evolved spiritually. Ultimately, you have decided on the life that the Divine has prepared for you.

You desire a successful life. From that moment you have decided on the desire and you have never changed your mind, not for a second. You have transplanted your burning desire into your mind to thrive and live life abundantly. You have filled your mind with successful ideas and let the nature translate this into the language your subconscious mind can understand and turn it into reality.

All these things happened in your mind by repeating every day the pledge that you are thriving. As time went on you have built enough self-confidence and belief there is nothing you can't have, desire and be. It is because you have connected the power of desire and back to **The Source**. Remember only with a strong desire and faith can this pull you out of difficult situations and rise from the horizon and flying like a phoenix. Never accept the possibility "*as is*" with faith you can fight the battle and win the war with **The Source** behind you.

There are hidden beliefs behind you preventing you from getting the desire you want in life. When these old subconscious thoughts are not being dealt with, they become the barriers and the reasons you don't have what it takes in life.

The fact is for most of us, we are unaware of their presence. Until these old subliminal beliefs are brought to your conscious awareness and you have no way of knowing where the true treasure is. Indeed, you have carried these old habits with you while growing up, as if you are wearing a pair of transition glasses and it filters everything automatically and stops you from seeing things as they truly are. So, you only see what is filtered in the unconscious hours that shadow your current sensitivity.

When you reside behind this screen filtered with untrue events and conditions you believe in and accept it as real, then your life remains to be covered in the mist. With the transition glasses on you'll never live life fully and successfully.

Imagine you are living in the screen of old belief that could prevent you from obtaining the treasure of true love in your dream life. You have a group of unwanted guests emerge at the door and your home has been invaded by them, because you don't have the power to stop them.

Let's take a look at these seven uninvited guests:
- old thought patterns, bad habits and attitude,
- past experience,
- fear, worry, anxiety, envy,
- your heritage, culture background, custom,
- negative emotions and feelings,
- something no longer serve the purpose and are still stuck in the mind
- prevent you from living the life you desire

Obviously, you are aware of their presence, because they have your silent consent to come into your home. You are being observed by them with their omnipresent. You are not acting as your real self because of feeling unloved, unless you have your house in order and consciously aware of the love within your heart and can aid you to rid of the uncontrolled situations.

You don't want to start the car engine with the foot on the brake and you know you are going nowhere. How many times have you done this to yourself? You need to have a strong conviction to make these changes so that you can enjoy your life. You can live life abundantly with the awareness of an infinite love and a peaceful presence.

Now tranquil and silent the mind, and find a quiet spot and begin meditation. Meditation is to help you attain the fulfillment and awareness with the oneness with the infinite self.

Your conscious mind communicates with the Universal Mind through the Inner Self. It is through the innate power, where clues or inspirations are received. Through this power new thoughts are given to you. These creative visualizations work well when the conscious mind is stimulated through the emotions of strong desires to succeed.

HERMAN WONG

Now imagine that you are sitting at conference table and surrounded by spiritual intelligences that are waiting to aid you in realizing your desire.

These spiritual guests will listen to you silently and bring forth ideas to you from them.

These spiritual guests are:
- Your spiritual heart—free from memories that hold you back
- Higher intelligence—the Source
- Your Inner Voice
- Your spirit—Who you really are
- Your alignment with the Source
- Your state of balance—emotions and feelings
- Living in your own reality
- Your inspiration

These are the invisible spiritual advisers that you want to connect and to assist you in your journey. You would like them to stay and aid you to manifest the dream you love. After you have experienced their present you will love to connect with them again!

Your heart is located in the center of your body. It is the most important core function of your being. While spiritual heart is the connection between the finite and the Source, which is your link to your dreams.

It is very intelligent and has the ability to understand, think and is full of love and peace. It holds the important source of guidance and wisdom and where your reality is. The *Higher Consciousness Self* manifests in the individual consciousness through the power of the Inner Voice, which can be heard by anyone who listens and recognizes it. Your *Higher Consciousness Self* is sublime and does not have any agenda's but only wants to assist you in your ongoing journey and will guide you smoothly and silently along the path and ultimately directs you back to **The Source**. The Higher Consciousness Self can and should always be trusted. The more you listen and recognize your Inner Voice gradually;

it will become an important source of guidance, intuition, and inspiration in your life.

Knowing your self is an extremely important to identify and recognize those aspects that are holding you back and taking action to eliminate or transmute those negative self aspects until your body, mind and spirit are aligned and accept only positive attributes. This may take courage, and acceptance during the long process, but the results are amazing, both in life and the continuing journey. Knowing yourself is learning and becoming aware of the truth, so that you do not judge others. People who judge others should remember that they should see themselves in others and love is allowed to express itself. Everyone should assist each other with unconditional love and provide genuine service to others without any thought for themselves for personal gains.

All your thoughts and actions have profound effects on your own reality and all those around us, because of our Higher Consciousness Self is connected with each other and the Source.

Rather than just thinking positive or manifesting desire continually or try to heal illness to yourself or others, or to eliminate discomfort and negative thoughts, you must be still to realize that in each moment you do not have to be concerned with the outcome to have profound positive effects and benefits. By practicing daily meditation you listen to the *Inner Voice* for clues and objective reasoning that will allow you to be free from worry, so that all your desires will be manifested to benefit your life and receive its bountiful benefit of health, wealth, success, and gradually this will become your own reality.

By being aware of this, you have taken full control over your thoughts by focusing on your needs will improve quality of life, which brings about the vibrational harmony and aligned with the abundant infinite Universe.

The pressure and problems in the physical world will no longer have any effect on you, knowing that you have complete control over your destiny and you are removed from danger and you are free from harm.

Remember each and every one of us has the power to create and control over our own reality. Although someone might seek to affect your destiny, but only you alone can ultimately control the horizon and vertical thus ensuring that the external influence cannot affect your life. Belief in yourself enables you to take the right action at the right time and in the right place to create a successful reality. Luck and success come, shall always stay with you, and believes you have the right substance to create your own reality and focusing on positive thoughts, you have channeled this energy to resonate with time, place and consciousness.

When you focus on the now and your energy is transfixed only on what should transpire to create that moment of success. Therefore, you experience luck and success in the present.

You deliberately chose positive thoughts and emotions stay in the higher energy field and will bring more love, abundance, and wealth to you. Furthermore, you must trust and have belief in your own ability to win the huge results and unify everything to your world.

Do you spend time with your desire?

Let's assume that you desire to find love in your life within the next two years. But, did you spend enough time to manifest your goal? When at the end of the day you realize that you have not spent time on addressing your goal, then you have a misalignment and less likely you reach your goal. As soon as you recognize it and adjust accordingly.

You need to take the right action to where you want to be, to have and to desire and make sure you have added emotions to your goals accomplishment. Your goal must have value then you receive it because of your strong conviction and belief in yourself and the goal. Don't get discouraged, if nothing happens after a period of time, but face it consciously and look around to see any changes. Changes may already have occurred in your thinking and behavior. You may have set things in motion that you can't see it as yet. Ennui sets in when you assume things or events didn't happen with your thought. So, accept the obstacle and let it fade out, and continuously aligned with your Source and expect your goal is here. You can see it and feel it with your whole being. Especially, when the whole envision comes from your authentic and centered place, this has unlimited potential for you to fulfill your dreams and desires. Now take a long deep breath, tranquil the mind and feel the transformational changes in that instant and consciously aware of each moment has the potential for greatness, and sense the peace of the inner light so that the innate wisdom can be fully expressed.

Recognize your own strengths and talents are essential steps to strengthen any success you involve yourself in. It is your foundation. It is a unique gift inborn in you that can be used daily. You are asked to nurture and use it accordingly to guide your life.

This is the everlasting happiness you truly give to yourself and by being conscious of your real abilities and strengths; you don't need to feel with something else in order to fill the void. The emptiness will be filled by your own natural ability and mental powers.

Realizing your own potential and reaching for greater height in your desires, you begin to see the concept of sustainability in our world is not too far to reach and every dream comes true, because of your chosen life style, and living your dreams to the fullness.

Having stronger belief in you and living a purposeful driven life by focusing on the energy that sustains your success. It will act as a guiding light and encourage you to have greater hope and optimism in your mind. Therefore, it is important for you to check every moment to ensure that you are remaining focus on creating thoughts of abundance. Belief is an act of faith accepted by the mind that your dreams can be accomplished and the intent that brings you forward to achieving and manifesting all your desires. You have every potential to transform your dreams into physical trueness. Practice manifesting abundance everyday for happiness, joyfulness and the fulfilling experiences. Success is made of hope and belief that can bring much more power to make your dreams a dominant reality.

~the end~

Afterword

Success will only be cost effective if in your belief system there is strong faith and trust you will have success "*Now.*" In fact, it's here already. It's your peaceful ally. Nobody can give you this ultimate success that you always wish for.

People around the globe are working together to improve their ways of life. You work hard and diligently towards success and living abundantly. Therefore, you desire to attract more money into your life. It is your birth right to desire more money. You deserve abundance flowing to you and manifested in life all that your ask for.

Think about what it takes for you to live a dream life. I think of money, wealth, and riches. What do you think of that will bring your dreams to life?

So, what is money? Money is a source of energy that can be used to buy a luxury car, a beautiful house, going on vacation, beautiful jewelry, clothes, and to help others to improve their quality of life. So, where does this energy come from? How do I get more of this energy? This energy is coming from an internal source dwelling within you. You must let yourself open to receiving it.

But, I don't feel I am receiving more money into my life. Why?

You consciously desire money, but deep inside your feelings may not be in harmony disrupting your thoughts of money coming to you. Your thoughts and ideas are in misalignment with your Inner Source. Your conscious and subconscious minds are not in agreement with each other.

Therefore, you need to impress upon your subconscious mind to be in alignment with your conscious state. The conscious mind gives direction and the subconscious mind carries out the command. It is like the genie said, "*Your wish is my command.*" The subconscious is your *genie*.

242

High influential energy will increase your self-confidence because you are allowing this energy to ignite your thought to bring wonderful things to enter into your life. You look after your body, mind, and spirit with good nutrition, diet and plenty of exercise, and most importantly, you apply positive thought in your life. Because, when you are vibrating higher energy you are in a state of contentment and feel energized and powerful. The vibration of your desire and beliefs are in similar vibrational alignment. You can ask for anything to flow through into your creative experience. You can look into your current situation to make any transformations. When your desires are met, it shows that you're internal and external consciousnesses are responding to your surroundings and circumstances. You look at the external world full of kindness, truthfulness, caring and you do not project any unpleasant feelings, but are in touch with the power of the flow of love.

Self-confidence is extremely important in every aspect of our lives. Your embodiment has an enormous impact on how others perceive you. Although you're social skills, physical appearance may not be up to par, but that does not prevent you from being who you are and revealing your true abilities. You are a unique individual and your beauty is dwelling inside and reflects to the external state of mind. You can build on a strong confidence to do what you desire and gain success.

When your self-confidence is high you answer questions assuredly and are not afraid to admit you did not know everything. When your spirit is high, you can inspire confidence in others. Gaining the confidence of others is one of the key ways in which you gain financial success and wealth. You act and speak with authority and draw attention to you effortlessly and automatically. You use imagination to create a strong visualized image of what you could feel and experience to achieve your goals. When your passion and confidence is high and focused, you always approach things with positive attitude, staying calm and being patient. Your success will have a real solid foundation. You promise yourself that you are absolutely committed to your journey and to the end. You center your attention on the desires and allow the energy to freely flow through you according to your choices. You are not interfering with the flow of your creation and there is no need to be perfect, but enjoy the ongoing process and doing it effectively.

You can implement the power of confidence into whatever inspires you. Your faith, self-assurance, and positive attitude will help you to calculate the power of success and reach every goal effectively and confidently. You show people that you can lead them to a successful path. You are the candidate of their choice because of your demeanor, self-assurance, enthusiasm and a passionate interest to lead them all the way to succeed and improve their lives.

Your self-confidence will shine, and your soul appreciates you. This is because you always take the initiative in any situation without suppressing it. A person who has leadership quality will have the quantity of confidence in his blood stream and the soul desire to do the ultimate best. You know your purposes and unlock the gate to become the primary leader in your profession to lead and do what's right for the soul.

When you process from higher energy, you are more interested in everything, than just responding to an ordinary life. You wish to seek the truth. You do research until you get an answer. You refuse to accept life is just flat. You believe there must be something more than just living a standard life. You have your soul urging and drive you to go beyond. Every event in your life guides you through spiritual evolution. Now you want to seek a deeper truth about spirituality. You wish to understand more about spirituality and the inner source. You are questions and at first you feel perplexed and puzzle. Inner life is complex and unclear to you. Spiritual exploration is never a straight line. It changes from stage to stage. Then, one day after months of reading and research, finally, you are awakened. You stop seeking, and then you realize it is from within. The Inner Source is dwelling in your spiritual heart. You realize life's purpose is connected with God to spread God's peace on Earth. Letting people know they are not separated from their creator and peace is obtained from within.

You realize you live in a dream land where everything comes to light through the power of imagination. The imaginative power is coming from your creative thoughts, where you can create a visualized picture in your subconscious mind with a positive attitude and focused attention to gain success of your desires. It is a joyful event that you can perceive every step of your inventions through the power of thought and consciously is in harmony with the Universal Mind and brings success of your desires to light.

People with leadership quality and self-confidence know how to use their inner abilities to resolve problems that face them. This aptitude will direct him towards a steadfast action in resolving the catastrophe and transform them over to triumph.

When you understand the power of enthusiasm, you will understand that balance in life is very important. If enthusiasm is the emotions igniting you into action, then the mind power is the balance of your enthusiastic outlook. This is when you are whole-heartily devoted to an idea or action, because you have a disciplined mind. A natural leader knows how to implement the quality of his keenness and exercises endurance in time of turmoil and uses his self-control and eagerness to make a quick and accurate decision.

It is a true fact that the powers and the abilities inherited in our mind are practical and unlimited. This innate power is given to us before we arrive here. In fact, this power is the power of thoughts. Through this energy many incredible creations will continue to emerge by the *power of thought.*

The Bible taught us forgiveness and loves each other. In fact, it taught us to learn endurance, love, and peace. Forgiveness is a healing process to our body and soul. True forgiveness comes from the spirit within us. Until our mind is renewed, until we are enlightened with the spirit there remains a resistance, and this enmity between us and God that governs our every decision.

We know when we infuse energy of either optimism or pessimism will eventually emerge in our lives. The Invisible Universe and our subconscious mind can't distinguish from positive or negative and they treat fear and enthusiasm equally. If we insert energy in this matter, then we are submitting our request for it. Therefore, it is important to be aware of what you submit is always positive, but not the opposite.

You are aware of your physical body is composed of mind, body and spirit and we are an infinite being. Our souls have no shape. When your subconscious mind and vibrational thoughts are connected in a deeper level that is where you can feel **The Source**.

Blunders and failures are inescapable, because it helps us to progress and improve the quality of our lives. You ask your higher power to help you to give you the ability to fix your mistakes and then move on. There are reasons that cause failures to an invention. However, if there are no mistakes then there will be no progress. Failure does happen during experiencing of inventing. So, don't give up until you have seen success again!

Practice truthfulness, benevolence, tolerance, and integrity will enlighten your life to reach the apex of the pyramid of fulfillment. When you meditate on these four reflective words Truthfulness, Benevolence, Tolerance, and Integrity after a period of time and you will feel the difference inside and outside.

The Law of Karma states that if you do good thing to others then good things will return to you. However, if you go out and do something bad to others, then you will attract many unpleasant events to happen to you. By knowing this Law you want to use the power of your mind responsibly and wistfully.

The Power of Love is the foundation that the Universe is built upon in God's love and image. Love is energy and has substance, which can be felt. Love is the acceptance of one-self or others. Everything is unified and working in harmony with it.

If we want to get what we desire, we must open ourselves to receiving it. We can't just say to the Universe we want something, we must be willing to receive it. By working in harmony with the Law of Allowing we are telling the Universe that we are ready to receive what we deserve.

Finally, if you want to live a successful and abundant life you must follow the Nature of the Universal Laws. It will bring many success and abundance into your life. Let it continue to be part of you and use it wistfully and experience the joy in your heart for many years to come.

~The Unknown~

Our purpose is to experience life. To experience life we need to make choices. What choice we make determines our life experiences.

Word about the Author...

 Herman Wong was born in Hong Kong, where he spent twenty-nine years of his life. After obtained a business management degree from Cornwall, England, he went back HK and worked there until he was thirty, then came to British Columbia, Canada. When he was forty-eight, a profound spiritual transformation took place dissolved his old identity and radically changed the path of his life.

He dedicated his time to comprehending, integrating, and deepening that transformation, which manifested the foundation of concentrating on a spiritual journey. Herman is not connected with any particular religion or tradition. In his path, he is working on an effortless yet profound truth to seek his spiritual journey into the unknown to find God. However, he has awakened. He knows very well that a profound God dwells within him. He realizes contentment is the only way to eternity joy and happiness.

Recently, I asked myself, "What I can offer to the abundant Universe for all that I received..." I don't know the answer until I read what I have written on it.

Herman has now completed *"The Spiritual Medicine : The Power of Success."* He has lived in Burnaby BC, Canada to present.

Success is aligning with your inner Source to navigate the mind to a positive thought energy with a strong belief and faith to succeed, and transferring any area in your life to create the unstoppable flow of wealth and riches, and activating your motivational thinking to live for success, spirit-enriching life, passionate focus and enthusiastic outlook.

THE END